Rachel Andrew

THE NEW CSS LAYOUT

MORE FROM A BOOK APART

Accessibility for Everyone
Laura Kalbag

Practical Design Discovery
Dan Brown

Demystifying Public Speaking
Lara Hogan

JavaScript for Web Designers
Mat Marquis

Practical SVG
Chris Coyier

Design for Real Life
Eric Meyer & Sara Wachter-Boettcher

Git for Humans
David Demaree

Going Responsive
Karen McGrane

Responsive Design: Patterns & Principles
Ethan Marcotte

Designing for Touch
Josh Clark

Visit abookapart.com for our full list of titles.

Publisher: Jeffrey Zeldman
Designer: Jason Santa Maria
Executive Director: Katel LeDû
Managing Editor: Tina Lee
Editors: Lisa Maria Martin, Caren Litherland
Technical Editor: Chen Hui Jing
Copyeditor: Katel LeDû
Proofreader: Mary van Ogtrop
Book Producer: Ron Bilodeau

ISBN: 978-1-937557-68-3

A Book Apart
New York, New York
http://abookapart.com

10 9 8 7 6 5 4 3 2 1

TABLE OF CONTENTS

For Beth.

FOREWORD

GRAPHIC DESIGN ON THE WEB has evolved significantly over the past twenty-five years. At first, screen pixels were huge. Now they're so tiny we can't see them. We started with a palette of 216 colors, (if we had color at all); now we play in color spaces far beyond what's possible in any other medium. For years, typography was limited to a handful of typefaces. These days, we have more font options than metal typesetters would have dared to dream of. Layout, however, has barely evolved since the advent of CSS. Fifteen years ago, we created a layout for blog articles, taught it to each other, and pretty much stopped there. Frameworks like Bootstrap have given us a few more options but, even with responsive web design, we've been severely constrained by the limitations of our tools.

Now it's time to take a giant leap forward. It's finally page layout's turn to shine.

When CSS Grid shipped in March 2017, our toolbox reached a tipping point. At last we have technology powerful enough to let us really get creative with layout. We can use the power of graphic design to convey meaning through our use of layout—creating unique layouts for each project, each section, each type of content, each page.

Grid gets the most attention, but it's not the whole story. Combining all of the options available to us in CSS creates amazing new possibilities—it changes everything. Grid, flexbox, multicolumn, flow, writing modes, shapes, object fit, alignment, sizing, viewport units—these are the tools that now make up our full toolkit. They will make it possible to launch designs unlike those that have come before.

You hold in your hands a technical introduction to this new world, a practical tour of what's ahead. Absorb this CSS. Play with it. Don't just ship the same old layouts with a different underlying technology. Discover what has changed about our medium. Don't assume that we already know what the web is about to become. Or that web designers and developers have mastered anything about layout on the web. There is no "right way" to design layouts anymore.

Everything about web page layout just changed.

—Jen Simmons

1 WHERE WE CAME FROM

SOMETIMES, IN FRONT OF ROOMS filled with developers who have never had to turn their hand to a font tag or a nested style sheet, I remark that my career on the web predates *Cascading Style Sheets* (CSS). As CSS celebrates its twentieth birthday, when I look back over my own history of learning and teaching CSS, I marvel at the fact that it has taken until 2017 to come close to cracking how to do layout on the web.

Before we start looking at the methods for creating layout on the web that have landed in the past few years, I want to revisit where we came from. Doing this historical groundwork is important, because many of today's assumptions about layout stand on the shoulders of what has come before.

HACKING AROUND THE LIMITATIONS

Early CSS layouts were a mixture of *floats* and *positioned elements*. A common pattern was to give the main content of the page a wide left or right margin, and then use absolute positioning to place the sidebar into that gap. This worked—until you wanted a footer on the layout and couldn't be sure the positioned item would not be taller than the main content. A lot of websites attempted to fix the heights of elements to cope with this; it wasn't unusual to discover a page with elements overflowing one another, especially if you adjusted the text size to make fonts larger than the designer expected.

Over time, we became better at layout. Online community-created resources like the Noodle Incident (http://bkaprt.com/ncl/01-01/) still exist, with examples of CSS layouts to copy and paste. These relics of our past remind me how far we've come in terms of the complexity of the designs we build—and yet how much we still lean on the techniques we developed back then.

As we became better at building floated layouts, we continued to be frustrated by the lack of full-height columns. Having floated a sidebar left and the main content right, there was no way to put a background color or image behind that sidebar. It would sit just under the content.

But web designers have always been incredibly resourceful at finding creative ways to use a limited toolset. A solution to the full-height column conundrum came when Dan Cederholm documented his "faux columns" technique on *A List Apart* (http://bkaprt.com/ncl/01-02/). By tiling an image behind the entire layout, we could create the *effect* of a full-height column.

That was just one of the many ways we learned to fake the appearance of layouts. The main debate—aside from a few outliers stubbornly insisting we should continue to use HTML tables for layout—revolved around whether we should build designs that had a fixed pixel width, or designs that stretched to fill the available screen space (sometimes referred to as *liquid* designs). Those of us who developed and taught these techniques got pretty adept at them, and knew how to identify most of the tricky browser bugs we had to work around.

Then came a curveball: the iPhone. As the web community discussed the best way to provide a separate mobile site, Ethan Marcotte set forth his ideas on responsive design (http://bkaprt.com/ncl/01-03/). A whole new challenge for CSS layout materialized.

By the time Marcotte detailed his responsive design ideas on *A List Apart*, many websites had already opted for a fixed-width approach. Larger screens meant that liquid websites stretched too wide, and reliance on methods such as faux columns made it very hard to create flexible grids. Responsive design threw everything up in the air again—not only did we need to create designs that used fluid percentage-based grids, but we had to do so for a multitude of screen sizes. The techniques we had developed fell apart, and we had to revisit how we used floats and other parts of CSS to make layout easier.

THE TROUBLE WITH FLOATS

Floats have served as the main method for achieving multiple-column layouts since the early days of CSS. When you float an element, it will, as its name suggests, float up to the left or right as far as it can go. It stops when another element blocks it. Floats were initially designed to achieve a common design pattern where text wraps around an image or other element (**FIG 1.1**).

If you float two items, then, the second element will float up alongside the first, assuming the parent container is wide enough (**FIG 1.2**).

This is the behavior we've been using to create our multiple-column layouts with floats. If we precisely calculate the widths of our floats inside a container, we can float columns up alongside each other. This works quite nicely if all our content is the same height (**FIG 1.3**). The code looks like this:

```
.cards {
  margin: 0 -10px;
}
.cards li {
  float: left;
  width: calc(33.333333333% - 20px);
  margin: 0 10px 20px 10px;
}
```

 No account of the early history of English aeronautics could possibly be complete unless it included a description of the Nassau balloon, which was inflated by coal-gas, from the suggestion of Mr. Charles Green, who was one of Britain's most famous aeronauts. Because of his institution of the modern method of using coal-gas in a balloon, Mr. Green is generally spoken of as the Father of British Aeronautics. During the close of the eighteenth and the opening years of the nineteenth century there had been numerous ascents in Charlier balloons, both in Britain and on the Continent. It had already been discovered that hydrogen gas was highly dangerous and also expensive, and Mr. Green proposed to try the experiment of inflating a balloon with ordinary coal-gas, which had now become fairly common in most large towns, and was much less costly than hydrogen.

FIG 1.1: A single floated element with wrapped text.

Code example: http://bkaprt.com/ncl/01-04/

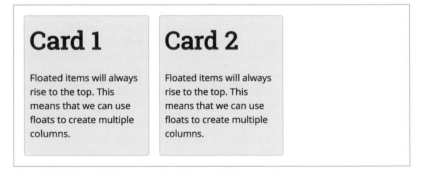

FIG 1.2: Two floated elements.

Code example: http://bkaprt.com/ncl/01-05/

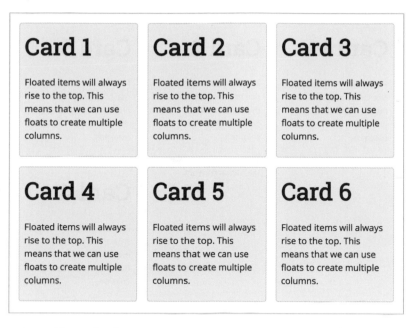

FIG 1.3: A tidy set of cards.

Code example: http://bkaprt.com/ncl/01-06/

As soon as we add some additional content to one of our blocks, though, we have a problem. The first three items, including the taller Card 2, lay out nicely. But Card 4 can no longer float past, creating some undesirable white space (**FIG 1.4**).

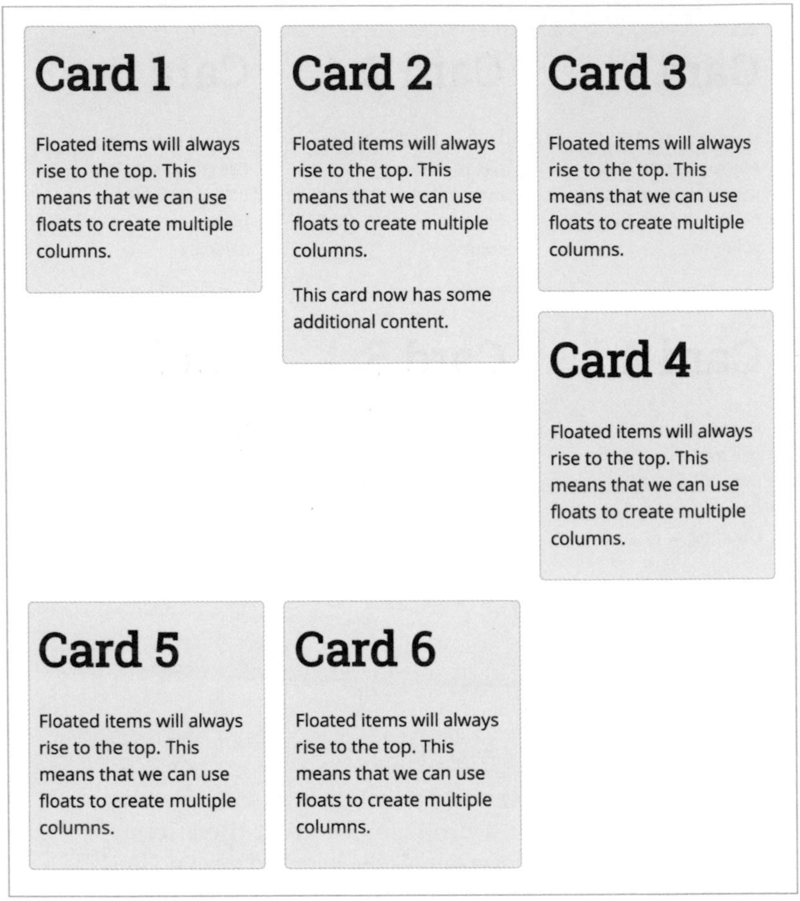

Card 1

Floated items will always rise to the top. This means that we can use floats to create multiple columns.

Card 2

Floated items will always rise to the top. This means that we can use floats to create multiple columns.

This card now has some additional content.

Card 3

Floated items will always rise to the top. This means that we can use floats to create multiple columns.

Card 4

Floated items will always rise to the top. This means that we can use floats to create multiple columns.

Card 5

Floated items will always rise to the top. This means that we can use floats to create multiple columns.

Card 6

Floated items will always rise to the top. This means that we can use floats to create multiple columns.

FIG 1.4: A messy set of cards.

FIXING THE FLOAT PROBLEM

The pragmatic solution many layout frameworks propose is to put each row of the grid in a wrapper, with a clearfix applied. This contains the floats and prevents any inhabitants of the second row from hopping up into the first row's space.

This works, but we then require additional markup to create our rows. An alternate solution is to use `display: inline-block` instead of floating the elements.

```
.cards li {
    display: inline-block;
    vertical-align: top;
    width: calc(33.333333333% - 20px);
    margin: 0 10px 20px 10px;
}
```

Code example: http://bkaprt.com/ncl/01-07/

Alas, this method comes with its own issues. If you set something to `inline-block`, it remains an inline element, but enables some additional block-like behavior. One aspect of being inline is that inline elements preserve white space; if they didn't, every word in a sentence would run together, since the spaces between words would not be maintained. If we use the same method to calculate the size of the item widths as we did for floats, we find that we only get two items on each row. The additional white space means our cards now add up to more than 100%.

The solution is to completely remove white space between our cards—which works, but can make for a slightly fragile layout (**FIG 1.5**). If any white space gets into the document—perhaps due to a change in the CMS or just a forgetful web designer—we'll end up with only two cards per line again.

Neither method enables the creation of a layout where the boxes take on equal height across the row. With our floated and our inline-block layouts, we can create neat rows with some compromises, but any background or border on items will only extend as far as the content does. This produces a ragged edge on our rows.

A legacy method for creating a multiple-column layout exists that can address this issue; it uses table layout on items that are not HTML tables.

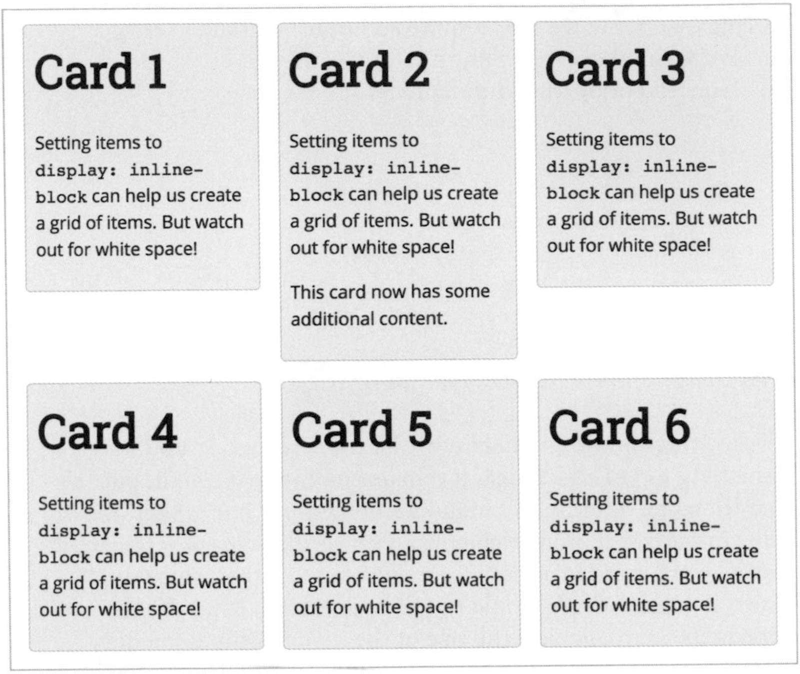

Card 1	Card 2	Card 3
Setting items to `display: inline-block` can help us create a grid of items. But watch out for white space!	Setting items to `display: inline-block` can help us create a grid of items. But watch out for white space! This card now has some additional content.	Setting items to `display: inline-block` can help us create a grid of items. But watch out for white space!
Card 4	Card 5	Card 6
Setting items to `display: inline-block` can help us create a grid of items. But watch out for white space!	Setting items to `display: inline-block` can help us create a grid of items. But watch out for white space!	Setting items to `display: inline-block` can help us create a grid of items. But watch out for white space!

FIG 1.5: The inline-block layout.

display: table

HTML tables have a related CSS specification—CSS Table Layout—that defines the properties and values available when styling this very specific type of structure. An HTML table has the CSS property display with a value of `table`. Inside an HTML table, we have `tr` elements (which have the `display` value of `table-row` in CSS) and `td` elements (which have the value `table-cell`). While these values were designed for styling HTML tables, they can be applied to things that are not, semantically speaking, tables—divs, lists, and so on.

To change the previous example to use Table Layout, we need to adjust both the CSS and the markup. I add a wrapper around the `ul` element and give it the `display` property with a value of `table`. This tells the browser that the contents of the wrapper will be laid out *as if they were* a table. Turning the ul element into a row causes the list items to lay out in one row. Therefore, I need to split the list into two lists and set the value of display on a ul element to table-row. The list items become table cells using the value table-cell.

```
.wrapper{
  display: table;
  border-spacing: 20px;
  margin: -20px;
}
.cards {
  display: table-row;
}
.cards li {
  display: table-cell;
  vertical-align: center;
}
```

Code example: http://bkaprt.com/ncl/o1-08/

Note that margins on our table cells and rows do not apply. To space out the cells, use the border-spacing property on the element that is set to display: table.

Because our items are now table cells, the background color stretches down to the same height for each cell, rather than sitting up behind the content (**FIG 1.6**). You can also use the vertical-align property to control the alignment of the content inside each cell—just as you can with an HTML table.

In our example, we have added elements for each part of the table, just as if it were an HTML table, giving an element display: table, a direct child of that element display: table-row, and ending with our individual list items having display: table-cell. In reality, you can often simply apply display: table-cell to an item and the browser will create *anonymous elements* to provide the other wrappers. We'll look at these anonymous elements in more detail in Chapter 7.

Table Layout works this way because items in a table have a *relationship*. This concept of creating relationships between

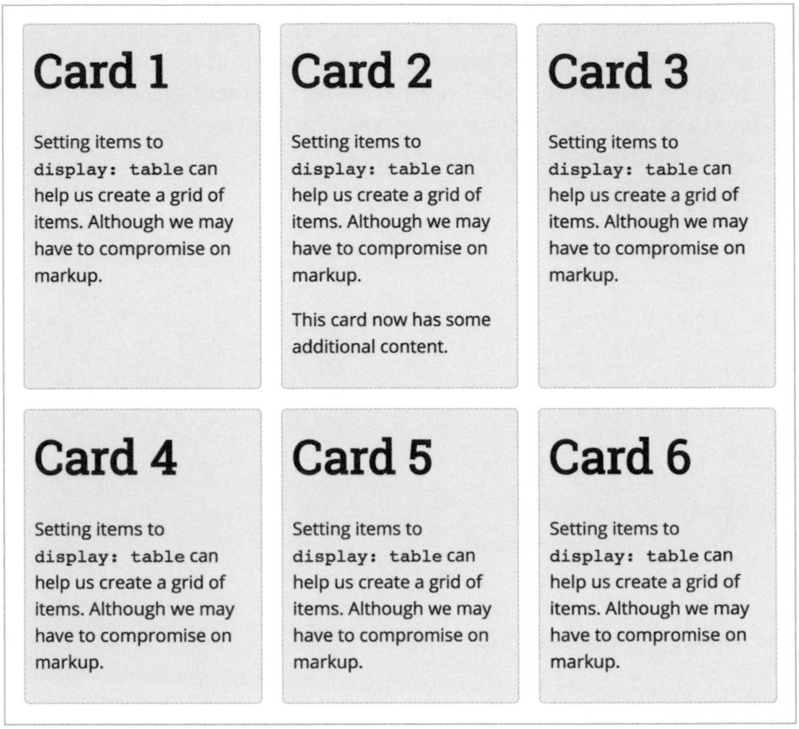

Card 1	Card 2	Card 3
Setting items to `display: table` can help us create a grid of items. Although we may have to compromise on markup.	Setting items to `display: table` can help us create a grid of items. Although we may have to compromise on markup. This card now has some additional content.	Setting items to `display: table` can help us create a grid of items. Although we may have to compromise on markup.
Card 4	Card 5	Card 6
Setting items to `display: table` can help us create a grid of items. Although we may have to compromise on markup.	Setting items to `display: table` can help us create a grid of items. Although we may have to compromise on markup.	Setting items to `display: table` can help us create a grid of items. Although we may have to compromise on markup.

FIG 1.6: The layout using `display-table`.

items in the layout is important in our newer layout methods, and we will return to it later in this book.

The techniques demonstrated in this chapter are our stock-in-trade as front-end developers. You will need to know these techniques for some time to come in order to deal with older browsers. Yet they are all essentially hacks that merely enable layout—not a designed-for-the-job layout system.

And that's why CSS layout seems hard and fragile—we don't have any layout tools! The fact that we've been coping with this situation for so long has led the community to create its own tools to ease the pain of layout. As we'll see in the next chapter, these tools have redefined what it means to be a front-end developer in 2017.

2 WHERE WE ARE

AS I MENTIONED IN Chapter 1, web designers and developers are an ever-resourceful bunch. Faced with spending a lot of time learning how to tame floats and coming up with other methods to enable complex web and application layouts, the community developed tools to help ease the way. These tools range from a raft of varying "best practices" in CSS architecture to pre- and postprocessors. They also extend to frameworks, and to the recent interest in design systems and pattern libraries, and working with reusable components rather than with finished pages.

In addition to a growing reliance on tooling, we are learning more about the implications of many of our choices in terms of performance and accessibility. The front-end development landscape of 2017 is complex and can seem overwhelming. This chapter will look at where we are today, to see how these new layout methods fit into the environment we have created.

Although the web-development community seems to love to polarize opinion, nothing that follows should be taken as an endorsement or condemnation of a tool or technique. Whether you should use any of these things is down to your individual project and team. What makes perfect sense for a team of fifty would probably be overkill for a solo developer. My aim is to assess the current landscape; whether you use these tools and techniques or not, the impact they have on how we do web design and development affects all of us.

CSS ARCHITECTURE

Programming style guides have been around for a while. Sometimes they stick to established principles; other times, they adhere to a common set of rules agreed on by a team. With formal CSS architectures, teams go a step further by adopting a methodology developed and promoted by an external person or organization. The various approaches to CSS architecture—OOCSS (http://bkaprt.com/ncl/02-01/), SMACSS (http://bkaprt. com/ncl/02-02/), BEM (http://bkaprt.com/ncl/02-03/), and so on—may seem like overkill if you are the only person who touches the CSS on the sites you build. Why make things so complicated? If you've ever had to work on a project where lots of people get their hands on the CSS, you soon realize why such architectures are useful.

Love them or hate them, these formal architectures have had widespread impact. Even small CSS demos are commonly created using BEM-style selector naming, making these systems part of the language around CSS. A side effect of these systems, and of the frameworks discussed later in this chapter, is that CSS has become more tightly coupled to the markup, with descriptive class names identifying how elements should look. These systems also promote less use of the cascade. Rather than identifying an element according to its position in the document tree, they encourage identification by class alone. This fosters reusability; however, critics might claim that the cascade is an important tool in reducing the amount of markup required for each page.

PRE- AND POSTPROCESSORS

Another part of the development toolchain in recent years has been that a growing number of people write CSS by *not* writing CSS.

A *preprocessor* is a tool like Sass (http://bkaprt.com/ncl/02-04/) or LESS (http://bkaprt.com/ncl/02-05/): you write CSS in a language other than CSS, and then compile to CSS. A *postprocessor* happens *after* you get to CSS—Autoprefixer (http://bkaprt.com/ncl/02-06/) is a good example of such a tool. Autoprefixer runs on your CSS file to add the required additional vendor prefixes for older browsers. It does this either on your handwritten CSS file or on a CSS file compiled by a preprocessor.

These tools are huge time-savers. Like formal architectures, they can help ease the pain of working with CSS on a team. One common way to use a preprocessor is to break the monolithic stylesheet down into smaller files so that people responsible for different parts of the application can work on individual files, which are then compiled. Pre- and postprocessors also enable maneuvers that, until recently, were impossible in CSS, such as setting variables for common colors, fonts, or sizing.

While these tools have had a net positive effect, they have changed the way many of us work with the core language of CSS. Instead of writing CSS every day, we write Sass. Having created our mixins for common tasks, we lean on those, rather than writing the actual end CSS that will be parsed by the browser. We're now a level removed from the actual reality of our CSS specifications—and we risk limiting ourselves to what our preprocessor of choice can do and thus missing some of the newer techniques that are becoming possible. Or perhaps we have postprocessors running and are unwittingly adding prefixes that are no longer necessary.

None of this is an argument against using these useful tools. Instead, consider it a case for remembering to take a look at the world outside of those tools once in a while.

COMPONENT-FIRST DESIGN

Formal architectures and preprocessors alike have helped enable a trend in web design of breaking things down into smaller components. Brad Frost has described this technique as *atomic design* (http://bkaprt.com/ncl/02-07/). Pattern library tools such as Pattern Lab (http://bkaprt.com/ncl/02-08/) and Fractal (http://bkaprt.com/ncl/02-09/) provide a framework for working with the hundreds of small components generated by working this way (**FIG 2.1**). A related concept is that of a *style guide* or *design system* (http://bkaprt.com/ncl/02-10/), a document detailing each component, separate from the complete pages that are ultimately generated from these pieces.

Such methods encourage us to look at design from the smallest elements outward instead of starting with a blank page and creating a complete design. Once again, proceeding this way has much to offer front-end developers who are part of a team, and can produce deliverables that designers working separately can hand off to the people who will implement the work. These methods constitute quite a departure from the early days of the web, when we typically thought in "pages" rather than in components.

FRAMEWORKS

Any discussion of modern web design invariably comes around to the fact that all websites look more or less the same. The chief culprit behind these "identikit" websites are frameworks—Bootstrap (http://bkaprt.com/ncl/02-12/) and Foundation (http://bkaprt.com/ncl/02-13/) being key players. These incredibly successful projects enable designers to quickly develop sites with minimal front-end knowledge. They also enable developers to create sites without needing an understanding of web design. A site built on Foundation or Bootstrap might not look unique, but it's less likely to look terrible than something made by a programmer.

Frameworks help mask a lot of the complexity that lies in creating float-based layouts. They do our calculations for us, so

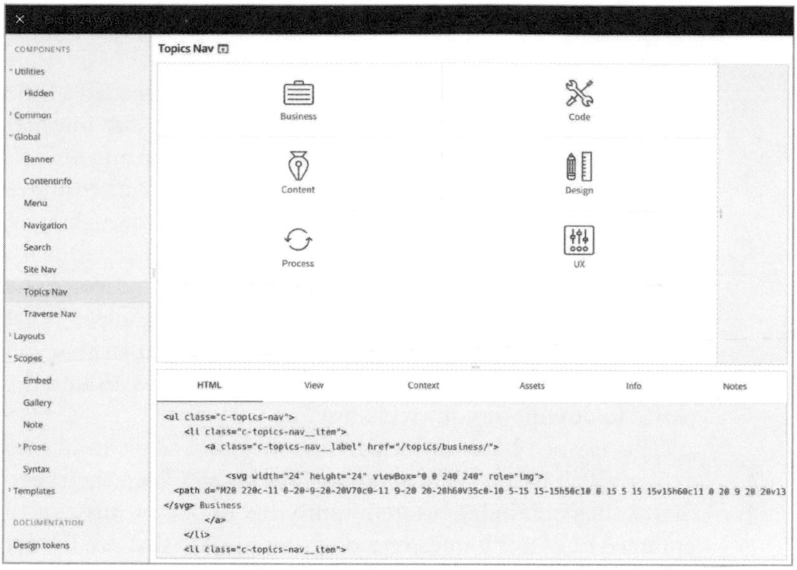

FIG 2.1: The 24 Ways component library using Fractal (http://bkaprt.com/ncl/02-11/).

we get the number of columns in the proportions we want at each breakpoint. We can look up the pattern we want to achieve in the framework documentation and copy and paste the code. But because many front-end developers rarely write CSS outside of these frameworks, they risk being unable to think outside of them. It's also worth remembering that all frameworks come with the opinions and requirements of what they were built for. These may or may not match your requirements.

PERFORMANCE

Another facet of life as a web professional is an increasing focus on performance. As we have tried to create websites that will look great on everything from a watch to a large retina screen, we have added an ever-increasing amount of code and images to our sites. The HTTP Archive reported that in December

2016, the average webpage download was over 2.4 MB (http://bkaprt.com/ncl/02-14/).

These large download sizes may mean that sites load a little more slowly for those of us at home or at work on fast internet connections, but they have a real cost for users on any kind of metered data plan. That might be me, visiting the United States and having to pay for expensive global roaming (though I can usually duck in somewhere with Wi-Fi). Of far greater concern is the person in a developing country, whose only access to the internet is via a phone on costly mobile data. Tim Kadlec's What Does My Site Cost? (http://bkaprt.com/ncl/02-15/) can give you an appreciation of what it costs people in countries around the world to download your website.

This is not a book about performance, but as we head into exploring all that is new in layout, we should keep the speed of our sites in mind. Let's make sure that in our enthusiasm to embrace new techniques, we don't build sites that are harder for people to use.

ACCESSIBILITY

And speaking of ensuring that everyone can use our sites and applications, the subject of accessibility can't be overlooked. Because of their capacity to disconnect the layout from the visual display and keyboard navigation, our newer layout methods also introduce potential accessibility issues. In Chapter 6, I discuss some of the powerful ways our new layout methods can disconnect the display order from the order in the document source. By giving us more power to rearrange our visual display, the specifications also require us to be more mindful of how we use it.

EVERGREEN BROWSERS

The existence of old browsers is a constant source of pain for web developers, and becomes an issue when large groups of users are "stuck" on some old browser version. We've seen this problem recur throughout the history of the web, with first Netscape 4 being the villain, then Internet Explorer 6.

For anyone running Chrome or Firefox, browser updates happen in the background, automatically. New browser features appear, and websites that take advantage of them will suddenly seem to be better. Safari and Edge update with operating system releases; users have grown more and more accustomed to running these updates to ensure for security reasons. They get a new browser at the same time.

Sadly, it is not as simple as everyone now having wonderful, self-updating browsers. A lot of our users do, yet we still see people chained to a browser version by internal policy. People also sometimes get stuck with a certain browser version because their operating system doesn't support newer software. Users of old versions of Windows may be unable to install IE11 or Edge. This problem increasingly crops up with phone hardware, too; think of Android users who can't update their OS, and therefore miss out on the new browser software that comes with the update.

Despite not having worldwide evergreen browser support, the situation has generally improved for most of us compared to a few years ago. It's worth implementing a feature that perhaps Firefox has shipped and Chrome has stated they will implement. Assuming the design will be online for a couple of years, a few months down the road, all Chrome users will see that enhancement. In Chapter 7, we'll consider modern ways of approaching browser support, and look at how we can create sites that enhance themselves as browsers update—without us needing to write any more code.

OUTSOURCING OUR UNDERSTANDING OF CSS

There was a time, perhaps ten years ago now, when the real job of a front-end developer was that of a browser-bugs expert. The CSS we had to work with was limited. What separated the professional from the dabbler was knowing all the strange tricks that prevented mysterious disappearing content in IE6. Today, our browsers are far less buggy, but we still have to contend with the limited CSS layout methods of the past, plus the new innovations of recent years.

We're also coping with the challenges mentioned in this chapter. We're trying to create performant, accessible sites that deliver on business goals and delight users. We're doing that work in every possible type of configuration—from the solo web designer who designs and implements her sites alone to huge teams where individuals only ever touch CSS at a component level.

There is nothing inherently bad about using a framework, a pre- or postprocessor, or any other tool to help ease your front-end development workflow. In the real world, we have to ship quickly, build things with unrealistic budgets, and deal with that client who insists a site look "the same" in IE8 as in the latest version of Chrome.

But if all your front-end development is in your preferred framework, how long will it be until you can't remember how to sit down in front of a text editor and build a layout from scratch? How do you find out about new approaches and new specifications? How much are you limiting your creativity to whatever the framework you use enables?

I hope that the rest of this book will encourage you to look past your favorite tools and frameworks to see what is now possible. Perhaps you will realize that you don't need to lean on the grid system built into a framework, or perhaps you will find yourself using it more lightly. I hope that however you build sites in the future, I'll be able to demonstrate to you some of the potential of CSS, and increase your understanding of why certain things happen.

3
THE NEW LAYOUT

AS WE START LEARNING how to use our new layout methods, we should also remind ourselves what the existing tools in our CSS layout toolkit are for. We've been hacking around with these things for so long that it's easy to lose sight of the functions they were originally designed for.

In this chapter, I'll run through the various methods we have for positioning items in CSS. You'll be familiar with some of these, but I ask you not to skip over what you think you already understand. These older specifications are still being developed, too; we are seeing new values for older properties and greater clarification of some of the magic behind CSS layout.

I'll also use this chapter to clarify some terminology and basic concepts that are part of CSS layout. Understanding some of the formal terms used in specifications can make it far easier to go right to the source when you want to find out how a particular CSS property or value will behave.

FORMATTING CONTEXTS IN CSS

The CSS Display specification defines the term *formatting context* like so:

> *...the environment into which a set of related boxes are laid out. Different formatting contexts lay out their boxes according to different rules. For example, a flex formatting context lays out boxes according to the flex layout rules CSS3-FLEXBOX, whereas a block formatting context lays out boxes according to the block-and-inline layout rules CSS2. (http://bkaprt.com/ncl/03-01/)*

We'll start by looking at something that you probably use all the time, though you may not realize why it works the way it does: *Block Formatting Context* (BFC).

Block Formatting Context

Creating a new BFC on an element allows you to create an independent layout environment for the children of that element.

A new BFC is created any time an element

- is the root element;
- is floated;
- has `position: absolute`, or
- has `display: inline-block`.

A new BFC is also created if the `overflow` property has a value other than `visible`. Flex items, Grid items, and table cells also establish a new BFC for their child elements.

We can see how this works by considering a very simple example. Let's say I have a container, and inside that container is a box.

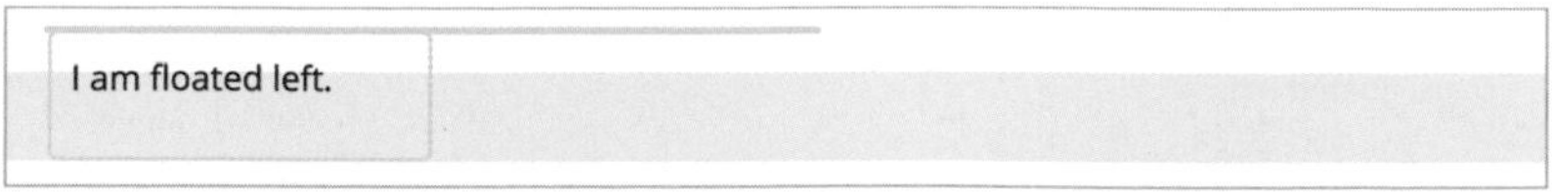

FIG 3.1: The outer container collapses because nothing is holding it open—the float is out of flow.

FIG 3.2: The float is now contained.

```
<div class="container">
  <div class="box">
    <p>I am floated left.</p>
  </div>
</div>
```

Code example: http://bkaprt.com/ncl/03-02/

If I float the box, the container collapses (**FIG 3.1**).

If I do something that causes the container to create a new BFC, however, it will contain the floats. I can do that in one of two ways. I can set overflow: hidden on the container:

```
.container {
  overflow: hidden;
}
```

Or, I can float the container (**FIG 3.2**):

```
.container {
  float: left;
}
```

I am floated left.

FIG 3.3: The container now acts as a new BFC, containing the float.

The element that has become a new BFC must contain everything inside it, which is why the overflow: hidden trick works to contain floats.

Because overflow: hidden wasn't designed as a clearing mechanism, it can cause issues like clipping box-shadows. So, given that creating a new BFC to contain floats has become such a frequent requirement, we now have a new value of the display property designed just to create a new BFC: display: flow-root. In browsers that support this new value, it forces a new BFC with no other unwanted effects. We can add it to an element such as our container from the previous example:

```
.container {
    display: flow-root;
}
```

Code example: http://bkaprt.com/ncl/03-03/

In flow and out of flow

When we floated the box inside our container (**FIG 3.1**), I explained that the container collapses because floating an element takes it out of flow. Elements that are in flow appear per their formatting model. The formatting model for block-level elements means they take the full width of the container (if not otherwise restricted) and appear on a new line. Inline elements display next to each other if there is room—just like words in a sentence.

If we float an element or set it to position: absolute or position: fixed, we take it out of flow. For floated items, this means the item moves up until it encounters a block-level element; following elements then move up alongside the floated item.

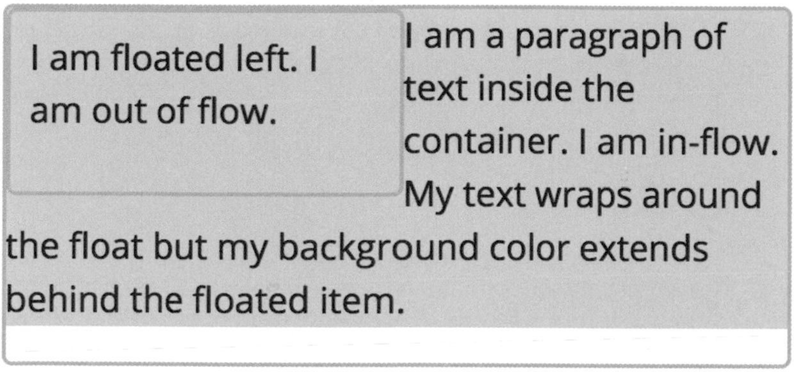

I am floated left. I am out of flow.

I am a paragraph of text inside the container. I am in-flow. My text wraps around the float but my background color extends behind the floated item.

FIG 3.4: The background on the paragraph displays behind the floated, out-of-flow item.

Note that while text appears to wrap around the floated item, it is only the line boxes that are shortened to wrap. If, as in the next example, you have a background color on a paragraph that wraps behind a float, the line boxes wrap, but the background color will extend behind the floated item (**FIG 3.4**).

```
.container {
  width: 400px;
  overflow: hidden;
}

.box {
  float: left;
  width: 200px;
}
.container p {
  background-color: #e5dbff;
}
```

Code example: http://bkaprt.com/ncl/03-04/

The other method we can use to remove an item from normal flow is the position property, which we'll look at later in this chapter.

FLOATS

In Chapter 1, I described the difficulties we encounter when creating multiple-column layouts using floats. Having moved to newer layout methods, you can use float to do the things that float was designed to do.

In my next example, I've decided I want to wrap the text around the side of the images—exactly what float was designed to do (FIG 3.5).

```
<ul class="icon-list">
  <li>
    <img src="../assets/images/aba-logo_small.png"
  alt="A Book Apart Logo">
    <p>...</p>
  </li>
</ul>

.icon-list img {
  float: left;
  display: block;
  margin: 0 10px 10px 0;
}
```

Code example: http://bkaprt.com/ncl/03-05/

Floats are also important if you wish to use the shape-outside property defined in Level 1 of the CSS Shapes specification. In this version of the specification, and in current browser implementations, you may only use shape-outside on a floated element. In my next example, I have a pleasingly circular image of a hot-air balloon. I've floated the image left, then used the shape-outside property with a value of circle(50%) to curve the text around the circle (FIG 3.6).

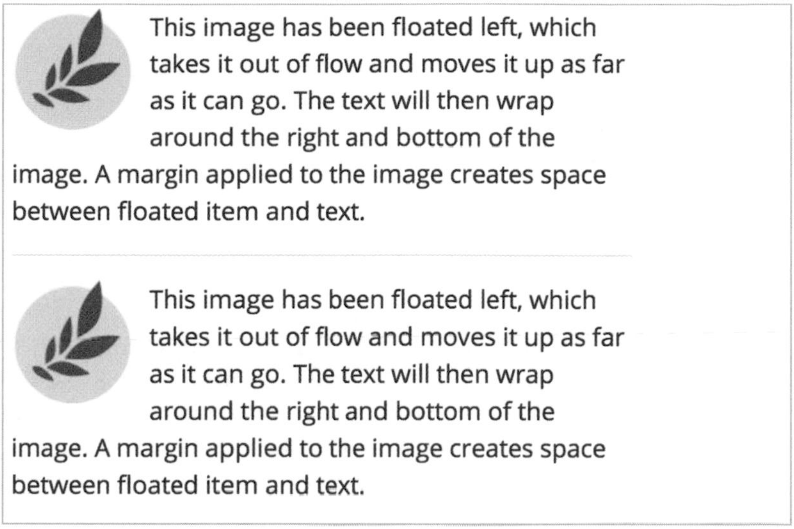

This image has been floated left, which takes it out of flow and moves it up as far as it can go. The text will then wrap around the right and bottom of the image. A margin applied to the image creates space between floated item and text.

This image has been floated left, which takes it out of flow and moves it up as far as it can go. The text will then wrap around the right and bottom of the image. A margin applied to the image creates space between floated item and text.

FIG 3.5: Floated items allow text to wrap around. This is still valid usage!

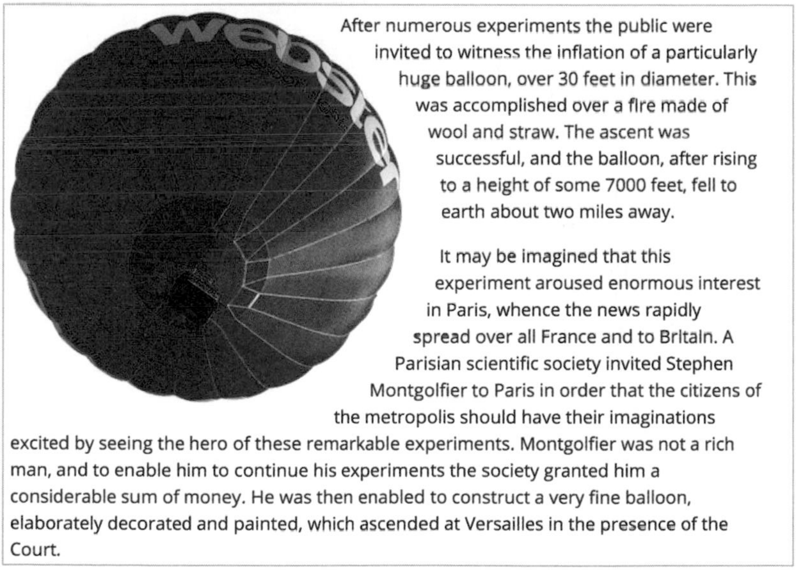

After numerous experiments the public were invited to witness the inflation of a particularly huge balloon, over 30 feet in diameter. This was accomplished over a fire made of wool and straw. The ascent was successful, and the balloon, after rising to a height of some 7000 feet, fell to earth about two miles away.

It may be imagined that this experiment aroused enormous interest in Paris, whence the news rapidly spread over all France and to Britain. A Parisian scientific society invited Stephen Montgolfier to Paris in order that the citizens of the metropolis should have their imaginations excited by seeing the hero of these remarkable experiments. Montgolfier was not a rich man, and to enable him to continue his experiments the society granted him a considerable sum of money. He was then enabled to construct a very fine balloon, elaborately decorated and painted, which ascended at Versailles in the presence of the Court.

FIG 3.6: The curved text created by combining a floated element and shape-outside.

```
.example img {
  float:left;
  display: block;
  margin: 0 10px 10px 0;
  shape-outside: circle(50%);
}
```

Code example: http://bkaprt.com/ncl/03-06/

If all goes well, our use of floats as a method for creating multiple-column layouts will fade away. Don't forget about the humble float, however—you can still include it in your designs. Using CSS Shapes can be a wonderful way to add a little bit of delight to the otherwise straight lines of many designs.

POSITIONING

The `position` property, in particular `position: absolute`, formed part of our early attempts to do CSS layout. If you used Dreamweaver back in the day, you may remember the ability to draw layers. These were absolutely positioned divs, and many people fell afoul of the overlapping content that resulted from building a website that relied on things staying the same height.

While absolute positioning may not be ideal for multiple-column layouts, it has its uses. There are also newer values of `position` that are worth investigating.

Static positioning

If you do not apply the `position` value to an element, it has the initial value of `static`. Items that have `position: static` display in flow, in document order. We only tend to use this value if we need to reset the position property on an element.

Relative positioning

Adding `position: relative` to an item does not cause anything obvious to happen immediately. If you add any of the offset properties of `top`, `right`, `bottom`, and `left`, you will find that you can push the element around from its default position.

This has limited usefulness. But `position: relative` has another advantage for us in layout: the item that has `position: relative` on it establishes a new *containing block*. This becomes helpful when looking at the next value of position, `position: absolute`.

Absolute positioning

An absolutely positioned item is taken out of flow, and can then be positioned from the edge of its containing block using the physical offset properties. In my next example, I have a container with a second box nested inside it. The inner box is set to `position: absolute`.

```
.container {
  width: 400px;
  height: 300px;
}

.box {
  position: absolute;
  top: 10px;
  right: 10px;
  width: 200px;
}
```

Code example: http://bkaprt.com/ncl/03-07/

The containing block in this example is the viewport, since there is no other parent element creating a containing block for this element. In my example page, this will make the box overlap the menubar!

If we want this box to be positioned inside the container, and to have the offsets calculated from the edge of the container, we need to establish a containing block on that container. We do this by adding position: relative to .container (**FIG 3.7**).

```
.container {
  width: 400px;
  height: 300px;
  position: relative;
}
```

I have set a height on my container. If I remove that height, the container will collapse, no longer respecting the height of the element inside. That's because the box has been taken out of flow, so it doesn't participate in layout decisions made by those elements.

Fixed positioning

When we absolutely position an item, it appears where we positioned it as the page loads. As the document scrolls, the element will scroll with the rest of the content. Fixed positioning enables items to assume a fixed place on screen as the document loads, and then stay in that place instead of scrolling with the rest of the page.

A fixed-position box also uses physical offsets, which position it in relation to the viewport. In my next example, I have a fixed-position box that is one hundred pixels from the top and sixty pixels from the right of the viewport (**FIG 3.8**).

```
.box {
  width: 200px;
  top: 100px;
  right: 60px;
  position: fixed;
}
```

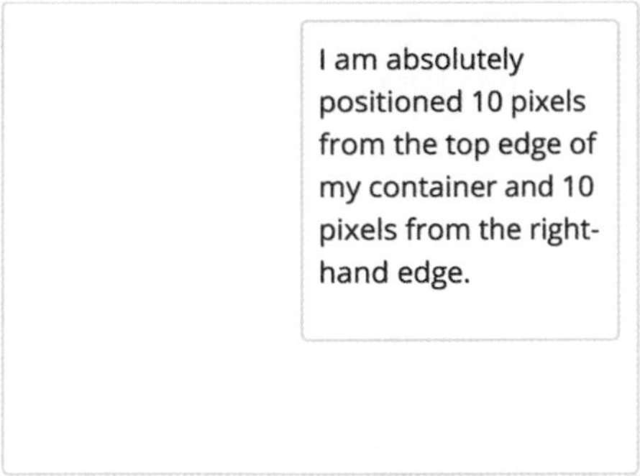

I am absolutely positioned 10 pixels from the top edge of my container and 10 pixels from the right-hand edge.

FIG 3.7: The absolutely positioned box is now offset from the container.

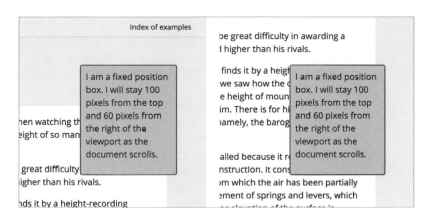

FIG 3.8: The fixed-position item always remains relative to the position offset from the viewport.

Code example: http://bkaprt.com/ncl/03-08/

As we scroll, the box remains in that position (**FIG 3.8**).

A common reason to use fixed positioning is to keep a menu on screen when scrolling through a long document.

Notice that the box is taken out of flow and so will overlap content, as in this example—if the viewport becomes narrower, there isn't a space in the margin for the box to sit in. If you don't want overlapping to occur, then you need to manage the layout so there is always a space for the box. This is typically the case for absolutely and fixed-positioned items; once the item is out of flow, you need to have a plan for how to deal with any overlap that may occur.

Sticky positioning

A newer value of `position` acts like a hybrid of static and fixed positioning. We already know that static positioning is the initial value for everything that loads on your page; static items are in flow and scroll with the document. We have also seen that items with fixed positioning stay in place relative to the viewport while the rest of the document scrolls. An item with `position: sticky` acts as if it is static until the document scrolls to a certain point—at which time it acts as if it is fixed.

In this example, I have a document with regular paragraph content in it (**FIG 3.9**). Also in the document is a box to which I've given a value of `position: sticky`. As the document loads, this box seems to have a static position. It appears in the document source before the paragraphs; in flow, the paragraphs know it is there and leave space for it.

```
.box {
  width: 200px;
  top: 20px;
  position: sticky;
}
```

Code example: http://bkaprt.com/ncl/03-09/

As we begin to scroll, the box scrolls in the same way as the paragraphs, which are `position: static` as they keep their initial value. Once the top of the box is twenty pixels away from the edge of the viewport, however, it "sticks," and the rest of the document scrolls while it remains in place (**FIG 3.10**).

As a newer method, sticky positioning has less support in browsers than some of the other values of `position`. It now

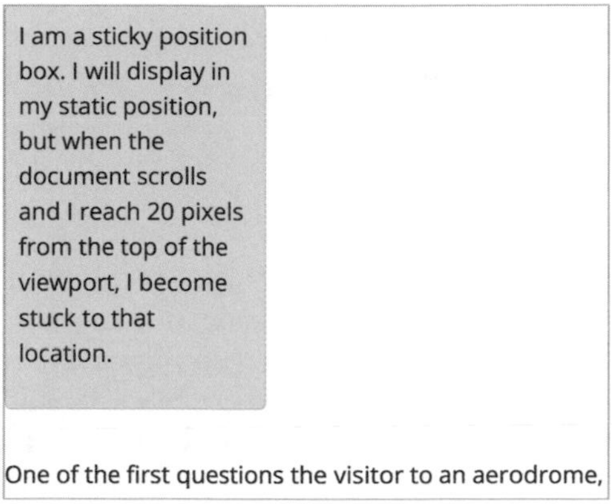

I am a sticky position box. I will display in my static position, but when the document scrolls and I reach 20 pixels from the top of the viewport, I become stuck to that location.

One of the first questions the visitor to an aerodrome,

FIG 3.9: The sticky box as the page loads, displaying in flow.

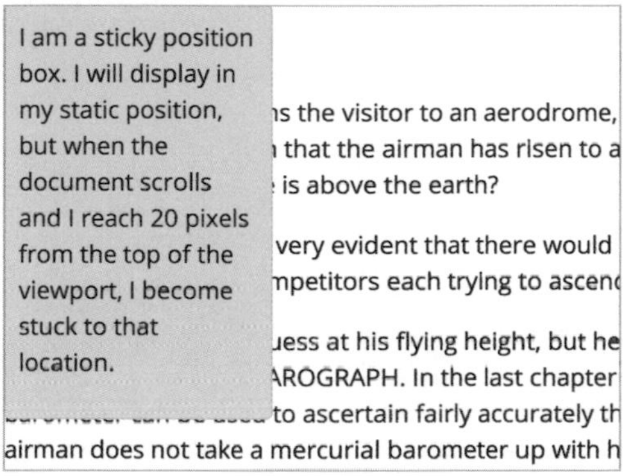

I am a sticky position box. I will display in my static position, but when the document scrolls and I reach 20 pixels from the top of the viewport, I become stuck to that location.

ns the visitor to an aerodrome, that the airman has risen to a is above the earth?

very evident that there would npetitors each trying to ascend

uess at his flying height, but he AROGRAPH. In the last chapter to ascertain fairly accurately th airman does not take a mercurial barometer up with h

FIG 3.10: As we scroll, the position box "sticks" once it reaches twenty pixels from the top of the viewport.

enjoys support in Firefox and Chrome, though, so it can be a useful effect for your pages. And, as something we have already been doing with JavaScript, it is relatively straightforward to polyfill; a quick search will turn up several available solutions.

If you decide not to polyfill, then the user will simply not get the nice sticky behavior—the element will remain in flow and scroll with the page. This is a great example of a feature that can be added as a nice enhancement without damaging the experience for users of older browsers.

MULTIPLE-COLUMN LAYOUT

Multiple-column layout is a method of splitting up a chunk of content into columns, much as you might see in a newspaper. At first glance, this doesn't seem to be an appropriate way to display things on the web. But there are good use cases for this specification, beyond making things look as they might appear in a newspaper.

Multiple-column layout is incredibly simple to use. To split content into three columns, I add the column-count property with a value of the number of columns I would like to have (**FIG 3.11**).

```
.example {
  column-count: 3;
  }
```

Code example: http://bkaprt.com/ncl/03-10/

Instead of asking for a fixed number of columns, I can instead ask the browser to display columns of around a certain width. For this, I use the column-width property; the browser will take my specified width as the ideal width for the column. The actual column may be wider or narrower than this ideal to account for the space available in the container. If you add a column-width and a column-count, the column-count will be treated as a maximum number of columns—even if the screen gets wide enough to accommodate more at your requested width.

```
.example {
  column-width: 300px;
  column-count: 3;
}
```

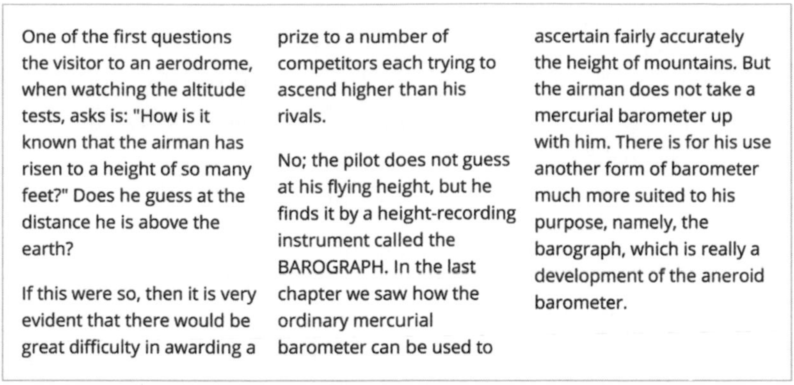

One of the first questions the visitor to an aerodrome, when watching the altitude tests, asks is: "How is it known that the airman has risen to a height of so many feet?" Does he guess at the distance he is above the earth?

If this were so, then it is very evident that there would be great difficulty in awarding a prize to a number of competitors each trying to ascend higher than his rivals.

No; the pilot does not guess at his flying height, but he finds it by a height-recording instrument called the BAROGRAPH. In the last chapter we saw how the ordinary mercurial barometer can be used to ascertain fairly accurately the height of mountains. But the airman does not take a mercurial barometer up with him. There is for his use another form of barometer much more suited to his purpose, namely, the barograph, which is really a development of the aneroid barometer.

FIG 3.11: Content wrapped into three columns.

This built-in responsiveness is a key part of multiple-column layout, and it was the first specification in which we started to see this kind of behavior. With `column-width`, we aren't able to dictate an exact pixel width. There is tolerance for the possibility of a container that is flexibly sized.

This specification is the only method we have that takes a chunk of continuous content and arranges it into a set of columns. Other methods act on the child elements, rather than flowing content regardless of what it contains.

One way I like to use this specification is in creating a more compact view of interface elements, such as a collection of checkboxes. By giving their container a `column-width`, I can collapse a long list into something that takes up far less room and requires much less scrolling. Using `column-width` means that the items display in two, three, or four columns depending on available space, without the need to control that with media queries.

This is a useful specification. It does a few simple things that can be very helpful if put to the right use. Try not to forget about it as a possibility when choosing which layout methods to use.

FLEXBOX

CSS layout really started to change with the introduction of flexbox, the Flexible Box Module, with features designed for a responsive, flexible web.

As the simplest flexbox example, imagine a list with three items in it (**FIG 3.12**). By setting the list to display: flex, the list items become flex items and start to take on some initial behavior of flexbox, spacing out in a row and stretching to the height of the flex container. All boxes are the same height, even though one box has more content inside.

```
.cards {
  display: flex;
}
```

Code example: http://bkaprt.com/ncl/03-11/

If we continue to add list items, then they will add to the number of items in the row (**FIG 3.13**). Ultimately, the row will overflow because the flex item cannot shrink smaller than its min-content size. In our case, the min-content size is defined by the longest word in the item.

To prevent this, we can allow our flex items to wrap onto multiple lines with the flex-wrap property.

```
.cards {
  display: flex;
  flex-wrap: wrap;
}
```

Code example: http://bkaprt.com/ncl/03-12/

The items will now stretch out and take up the full width; to see wrapping, we'll need to add the flex property to the items themselves. I'll explain this shorthand property and the individual components fully in Chapter 5. For now, know that we are allowing our item to grow and shrink from an ideal width of 200 pixels.

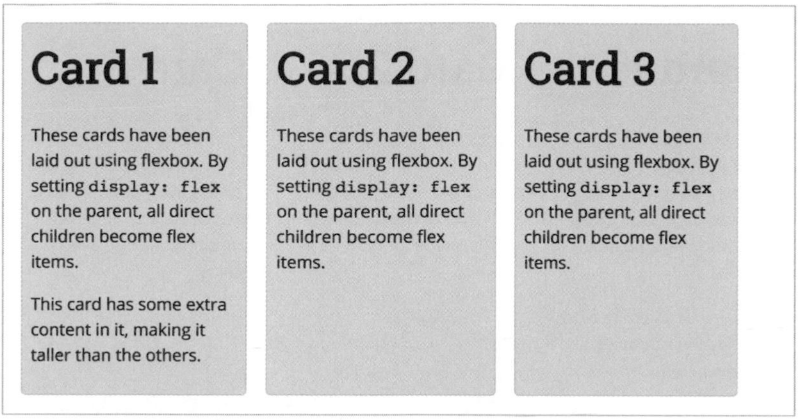

Card 1

These cards have been laid out using flexbox. By setting `display: flex` on the parent, all direct children become flex items.

This card has some extra content in it, making it taller than the others.

Card 2

These cards have been laid out using flexbox. By setting `display: flex` on the parent, all direct children become flex items.

Card 3

These cards have been laid out using flexbox. By setting `display: flex` on the parent, all direct children become flex items.

FIG 3.12: As soon as we add `display: flex` to the parent, the child items become flex items and start to use some initial values of flexbox.

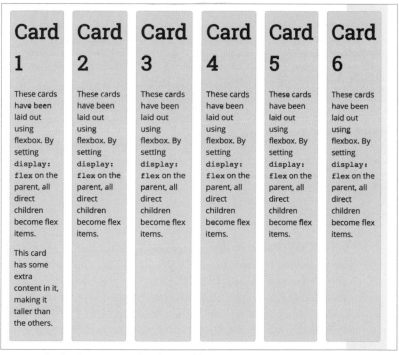

FIG 3.13: The flex items start to break out of the container.

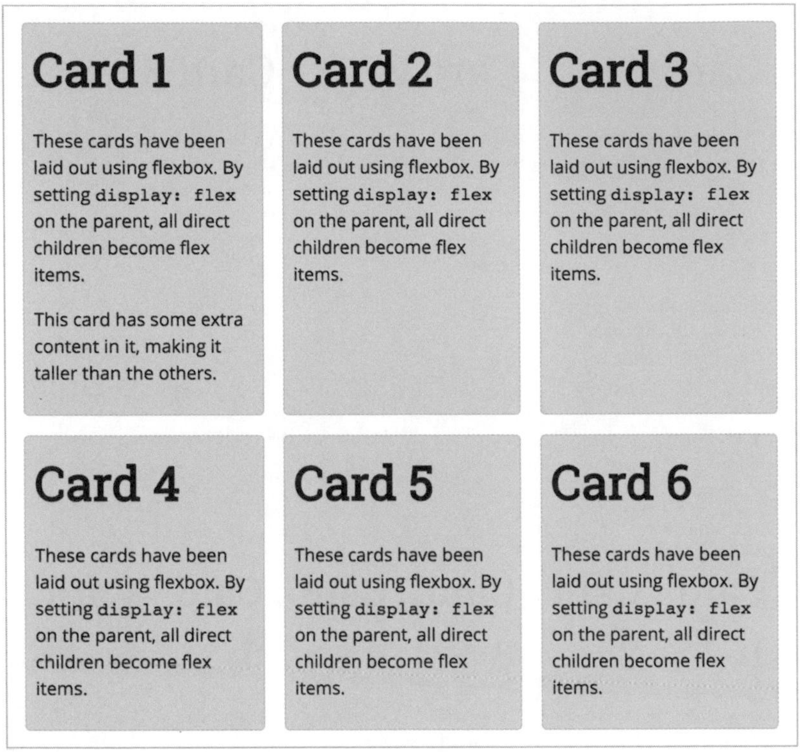

Card 1

These cards have been laid out using flexbox. By setting display: flex on the parent, all direct children become flex items.

This card has some extra content in it, making it taller than the others.

Card 2

These cards have been laid out using flexbox. By setting display: flex on the parent, all direct children become flex items.

Card 3

These cards have been laid out using flexbox. By setting display: flex on the parent, all direct children become flex items.

Card 4

These cards have been laid out using flexbox. By setting display: flex on the parent, all direct children become flex items.

Card 5

These cards have been laid out using flexbox. By setting display: flex on the parent, all direct children become flex items.

Card 6

These cards have been laid out using flexbox. By setting display: flex on the parent, all direct children become flex items.

FIG 3.14: Our items now wrap onto two lines.

```
.cards li {
  flex: 1 1 200px;
}
```

With six items in our container, the items wrap neatly into two rows and form a nice tidy grid (**FIG 3.14**). Don't be fooled! If we remove one item from the list, the grid effect disappears; the final two items share the space on the final row (**FIG 3.15**).

What happens when flex items wrap onto a new row (or column, if you are working with columns) is that the new row becomes its own flex container. This means that the assigning of available space happens across the individual row. Flexbox

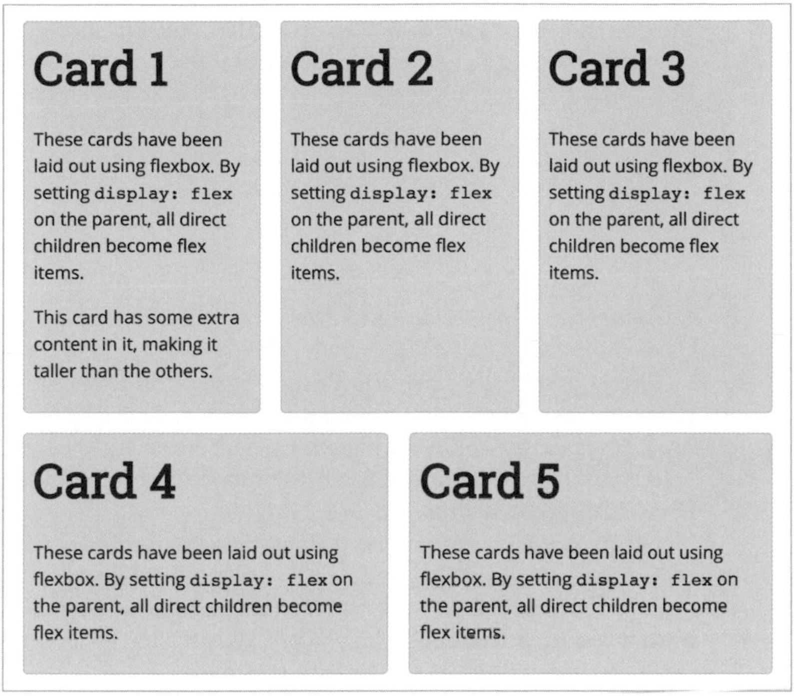

Card 1

These cards have been laid out using flexbox. By setting `display: flex` on the parent, all direct children become flex items.

This card has some extra content in it, making it taller than the others.

Card 2

These cards have been laid out using flexbox. By setting `display: flex` on the parent, all direct children become flex items.

Card 3

These cards have been laid out using flexbox. By setting `display: flex` on the parent, all direct children become flex items.

Card 4

These cards have been laid out using flexbox. By setting `display: flex` on the parent, all direct children become flex items.

Card 5

These cards have been laid out using flexbox. By setting `display: flex` on the parent, all direct children become flex items.

FIG 3.15: Distribution of space happens across the row—our final row now contains only two items.

won't try to line the items up with items in rows above or below. We describe this as *one-dimensional layout*. We are laying out our items in either a row or a column—we can't control both at once using flexbox.

To try to make flexbox behave more like a grid, we need to prevent some of the flexibility that is key to flexbox. In Chapter 1, we looked at a float-based layout that relied on our calculating the width of columns to make sure that they would fit into our container neatly. We can take the same approach with flexbox.

Give the flex item a width; then, in the value of the flex property, set flex-grow and flex-shrink to 0 and flex-basis to auto. Our boxes will not grow from the percentage width, which means that when we only have two items on the row, they do not stretch out and take up all the available space. As with our floated grid, we need to account for the gutter between items when setting our width.

```
.cards li {
  width: calc(33.333333333% - 20px);
  flex: 0 0 auto;
}
```

Code example: http://bkaprt.com/ncl/03-13/

This is essentially how any flexbox-based grid framework functions, using some variation on the above. These systems use flexbox for the ability to align things and create equal height columns, but avoid using the space distribution features in favor of calculating the widths.

In Chapter 5, I'll explain more about how the flex properties of flex-grow, flex-shrink, and flex-basis work. They can give you a lot of control over how your flex items behave. That said, if what you *really* want is a grid, you probably should be looking at the next specification on the list—CSS Grid Layout.

CSS GRID LAYOUT

As we have seen, flexbox wasn't designed for grid layouts—but this is where our newest specification is most at home. CSS Grid Layout does exactly what its name suggests: it enables the creation of grid layouts in CSS. This is *two-dimensional layout—* laying things out as a row and a column at the same time. We'll go over many more examples of Grid Layout in the rest of this book, but let's start by seeing how Grid can solve the problem we had with making flexbox display like a grid.

In this example, I'm creating a three-column grid (**FIG 3.17**). My container has display: grid, and I've created three equal-width columns with the grid-template-columns property, plus a new unit created for Grid: a flexible-length unit known as fr. We'll take a closer look at this unit in Chapter 5; for now, keep in mind that it represents a fraction of the space available

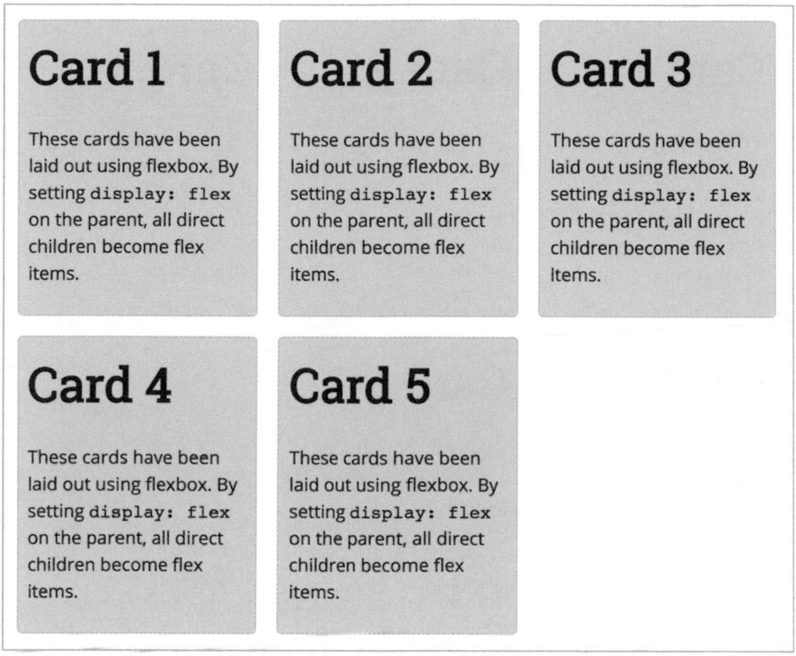

Card 1

These cards have been laid out using flexbox. By setting `display: flex` on the parent, all direct children become flex items.

Card 2

These cards have been laid out using flexbox. By setting `display: flex` on the parent, all direct children become flex items.

Card 3

These cards have been laid out using flexbox. By setting `display: flex` on the parent, all direct children become flex Items.

Card 4

These cards have been laid out using flexbox. By setting `display: flex` on the parent, all direct children become flex items.

Card 5

These cards have been laid out using flexbox. By setting `display: flex` on the parent, all direct children become flex items.

FIG 3.16: By preventing our flex items from growing and shrinking, then setting a width, we can make flexbox behave like a grid.

in the grid container. With three tracks all set to 1fr each, the available space is divided into three and distributed equally. This is all we need to do to get the direct child of the container to display as a grid. Unlike with flexbox, we don't need to add any rules to the children; they will just pop themselves into each cell of the grid.

```
.cards {
  margin: 0 -10px;
  display: grid;
  grid-template-columns: 1fr 1fr 1fr;
}
```

Code example: http://bkaprt.com/ncl/03-14/

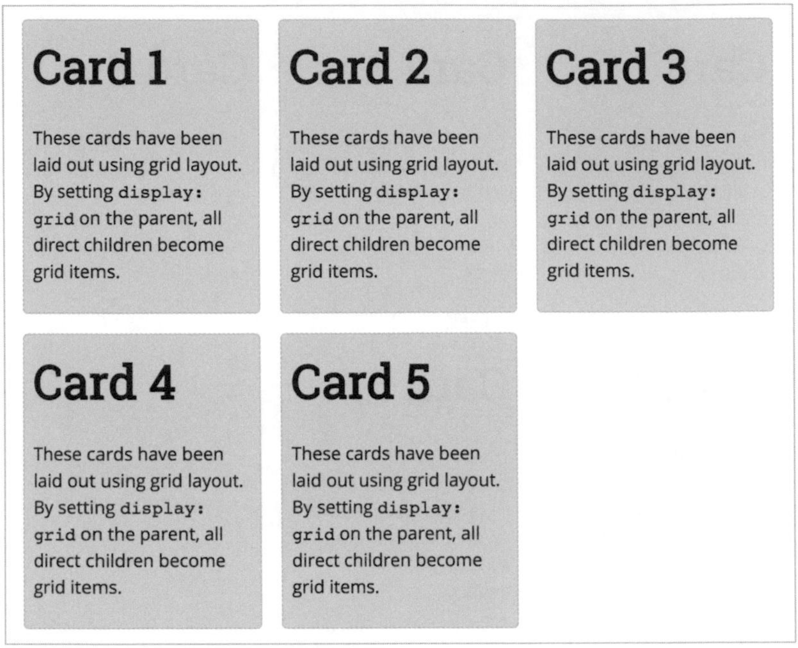

FIG 3.17: The basic grid layout.

As you can see, the items form a strict grid, without us needing to set any widths on them. We can solve another issue that we have with creating a flexbox grid, using properties that are part of the Grid specification. To create gaps between our flex items, in our flexbox example we used margins on the flex items and then needed to add a negative margin on the container to account for the unwanted left and right margin on the far left and right items. CSS Grid Layout includes a grid-gap property to space items out. This property is shorthand for grid-column-gap and grid-row-gap, which can also be specified individually.

To demonstrate how this works, I've removed the margins on the items and the negative margin on the container and spaced the items out with grid-gap. You'll produce the exact same layout as above in the browser, but without the need to mess around with margins and negative margins.

```
.cards {
  display: grid;
  grid-template-columns: 1fr 1fr 1fr;
  grid-gap: 20px;
}
```

Code example: http://bkaprt.com/ncl/03-15/

Just as this book was going to print, the CSS Working Group resolved to change the name of the grid-gap properties. grid-column-gap will become column-gap, grid-row-gap will become row-gap, and the grid-gap shorthand will simply be gap. In addition, the definition of these properties has been moved to the Box Alignment Specification. This means that in the future, flexbox may also support gaps in the same way as Grid.

Because browsers have already shipped these properties, they will alias the grid-* names to the new names for the foreseeable future. At time of writing, no browser supports the new property names, so I've retained the grid-* versions in these examples. If you want to be sure of supporting both versions, there's no reason not to list both in your CSS, as in this example:

```
.cards {
  display: grid;
  grid-template-columns: 1fr 1fr 1fr;
  grid-gap: 20px;
  gap: 20px;
}
```

Positioning items around the grid

We can quickly move away from what flexbox allows us to do by taking advantage of our two-dimensional grid and positioning items on it. The most basic way of doing this is by using line numbers. A grid has numbered grid lines; they start from 1 for both rows and columns. Note that these lines are numbered per the writing mode of the document. Working in English, a *left-to-right* (LTR) language, column line 1 is on the left-hand side of the grid; row line 1 is at the top. In Arabic, a *right-to-left* (RTL) language, column line 1 appears on the right of the grid. The far edge of the grid (right in a LTR language and left in a RTL language) is represented by -1.

```css
.cards {
  display: grid;
  grid-template-columns: 1fr 1fr 1fr;
  grid-gap: 20px;
}
.card1 {
  grid-column: 1 / 3;
  grid-row: 1;
}
.card2 {
  grid-column: 3;
  grid-row: 1;
}
.card3 {
  grid-column: 1;
  grid-row: 2 / 4;
}
.card4 {
  grid-column: 2 / 4;
  grid-row: 2;
}
.card5 {
  grid-column: 2 / 4;
  grid-row: 3;
}
```

Code example: http://bkaprt.com/ncl/03-16/

You can immediately see some of the power of Grid Layout here. We can span columns *and* rows—something that is hard

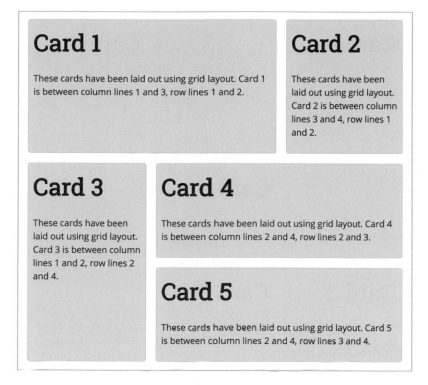

FIG 3.18: Cards placed on the grid by line number.

to do using existing layout methods. The background color of our cards extends to the gutter, even if the content is shorter. It's also very easy to change how far a block spans—we can even leave white space! If I change the start line of card 3 to row line 3, we get an empty cell (**FIG 3.19**). Nothing can rise and land in the grid cell; this differs from the behavior of floats, which try to float up and fill the available space.

Another method of positioning items on a grid involves using *named areas*. This allows you to describe your layout right in your CSS. To do this with our example, we first give each card a name with the `grid-area` property. I'm just using letters *a* through *e*.

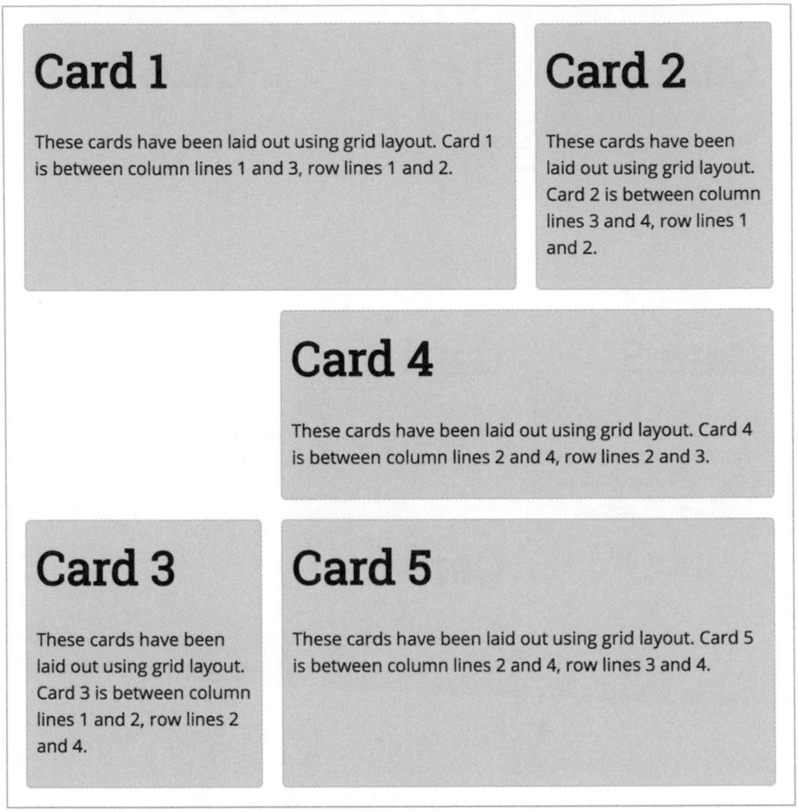

Card 1

These cards have been laid out using grid layout. Card 1 is between column lines 1 and 3, row lines 1 and 2.

Card 2

These cards have been laid out using grid layout. Card 2 is between column lines 3 and 4, row lines 1 and 2.

Card 4

These cards have been laid out using grid layout. Card 4 is between column lines 2 and 4, row lines 2 and 3.

Card 3

These cards have been laid out using grid layout. Card 3 is between column lines 1 and 2, row lines 2 and 4.

Card 5

These cards have been laid out using grid layout. Card 5 is between column lines 2 and 4, row lines 3 and 4.

FIG 3.19: White space made easy with CSS Grid Layout.

```
.card1 { grid-area: a; }
.card2 { grid-area: b; }
.card3 { grid-area: c; }
.card4 { grid-area: d; }
.card5 { grid-area: e; }
```

Next, I add the `grid-template-areas` property to the container. The value of this property describes what our layout should look like (**FIG 3.20**).

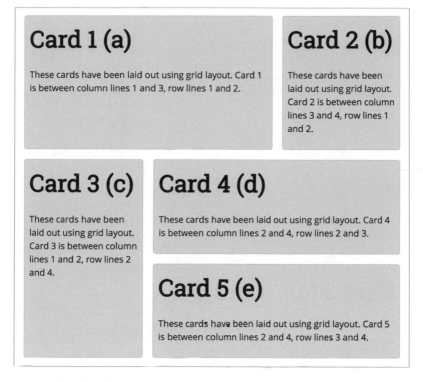

FIG 3.20: The value of `grid-template-areas` shows visually what our layout looks like.

```
.cards {
  display: grid;
  grid-template-columns: 1fr 1fr 1fr;
  grid-gap: 20px;
  grid-template-areas:
    "a a b"
    "c d d"
    "c e e";
}
```

Code example: http://bkaprt.com/ncl/03-17/

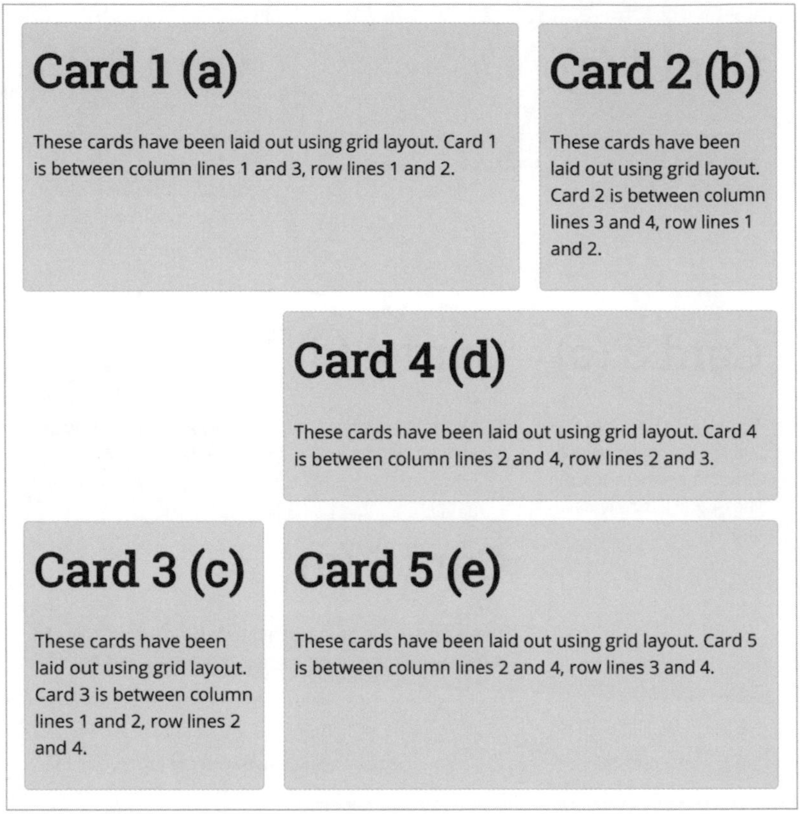

Card 1 (a)

These cards have been laid out using grid layout. Card 1 is between column lines 1 and 3, row lines 1 and 2.

Card 2 (b)

These cards have been laid out using grid layout. Card 2 is between column lines 3 and 4, row lines 1 and 2.

Card 4 (d)

These cards have been laid out using grid layout. Card 4 is between column lines 2 and 4, row lines 2 and 3.

Card 3 (c)

These cards have been laid out using grid layout. Card 3 is between column lines 1 and 2, row lines 2 and 4.

Card 5 (e)

These cards have been laid out using grid layout. Card 5 is between column lines 2 and 4, row lines 3 and 4.

FIG 3.21: We now have white space left in our layout.

There are a few things to keep in mind with `grid-template-areas`. To span across cells, we repeat the name of the area. Card 1 spans across the first two column tracks; thus a is repeated. The areas must be rectangular in nature—we can't yet create an L-shaped area.

To leave white space, and to leave a cell empty, use a full-stop character. If you replace the first c with ., that cell will remain empty when the layout is created (**FIG 3.21**).

```
.cards {
  display: grid;
  grid-template-columns: 1fr 1fr 1fr;
  grid-gap: 20px;
  grid-template-areas:
    "a a b"
    ".  d d"
    "c e e";
}
```

If your grid-area names are longer than one character, you may want to line up the visual rows and columns in the value of grid-template-areas. This is possible because more than one full-stop character can denote an empty cell—if they have no white space between them. You can also add more than one white-space character to space out grid-area names.

This is a very nice way to work with layouts, given how easy it is to move items around. I enjoy working like this during the prototyping stage—rather than worrying about how to achieve layout, I can figure out the best way for my interface to be presented. Then I can go back to the markup to make sure it's in a logical order based on those decisions.

With these few examples, you already have enough knowledge to start using Grid Layout, and to make decisions about which layout methods to use. There is more to come, but keep in mind that although the specification is large and can do a lot of things, it is very simple at its core. You can do a lot with very little CSS. As you start building layouts, you will have questions, and will want to achieve more with these layout methods. That's where the rest of this book comes in!

4 ALIGNMENT CONTROL

WE HAVE LONG LACKED the means to precisely align items in our layouts. Much of the excitement around flexbox has derived from this ability to stretch and align flex items.

In Chapter 3, I showed you some examples of flexbox and CSS Grid Layout. These specifications are pulled together by a third specification—the Box Alignment Module Level 3 (http://bkaprt.com/ncl/04-01/). This module takes the interesting and useful alignment features we find in flexbox and places them in a new specification, where they become available to other specifications. We currently see implementation of these features in CSS Grid Layout.

ALIGNING FLEX ITEMS

We've already seen how flex and Grid items stretch to the height of their grid area or flex container, giving us the equal-height columns we've always dreamed of! They can do this because the initial value of flex or Grid items is stretch.

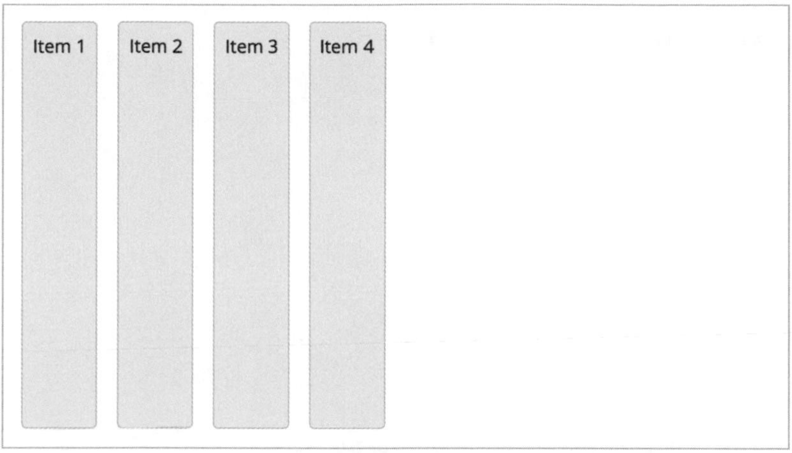

FIG 4.1: The items stretch by default because the initial value of `align-items` is `stretch`.

In this example, I have four flex items in a container (**FIG 4.1**). The container is set to `50vh`, and the flex items stretch to fill it.

```html
<ul class="cards">
  <li>Item 1</li>
  <li>Item 2</li>
  <li>Item 3</li>
  <li>Item 4</li>
</ul>
```

```css
.cards {
  margin: 0 -10px;
  display: flex;
  height: 50vh;
}
```

If we add the property `align-items` to the container, we can specify where the items will align with different values: `flex-start` will align items at the top of the container, `flex-end` will send them all to the bottom, and `center` will center them (**FIG 4.2**).

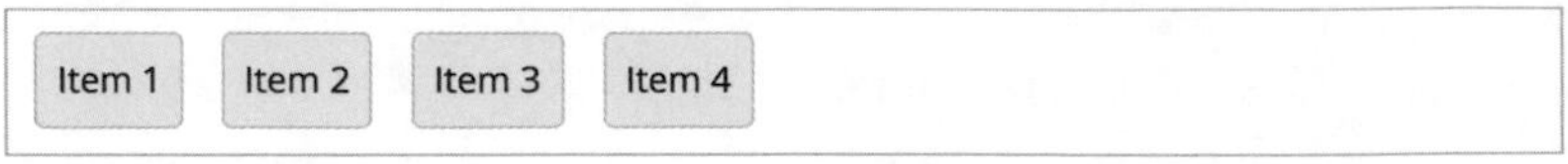

FIG 4.2: Use the `align-items` property to set the alignment of all items.

```
.cards {
  margin: 0 -10px;
  display: flex;
  align-items: flex-start;
  height: 50vh;
}
```

Code example: *http://bkaprt.com/ncl/04-02/*

The `align-items` property works on all the items inside the container. But you can override this by using the `align-self` property on an individual flex item. This takes the same values as `align-items`, but sets the alignment on individual flex items rather than on the group as a whole (**FIG 4.3**).

```
.cards li:nth-child(2) {
  align-self: stretch;
}
.cards li:nth-child(3) {
  align-self: flex-end;
}
.cards li:nth-child(4) {
  align-self: center;
}
```

Code example: *http://bkaprt.com/ncl/04-03/*

Alignment works on items on the *cross axis* (also known as the *block axis* in CSS, and as the *column axis* in the Grid specification). Our flex items are displayed as a row; the cross axis runs across the row vertically, stretching the height of the flex container (**FIG 4.4**).

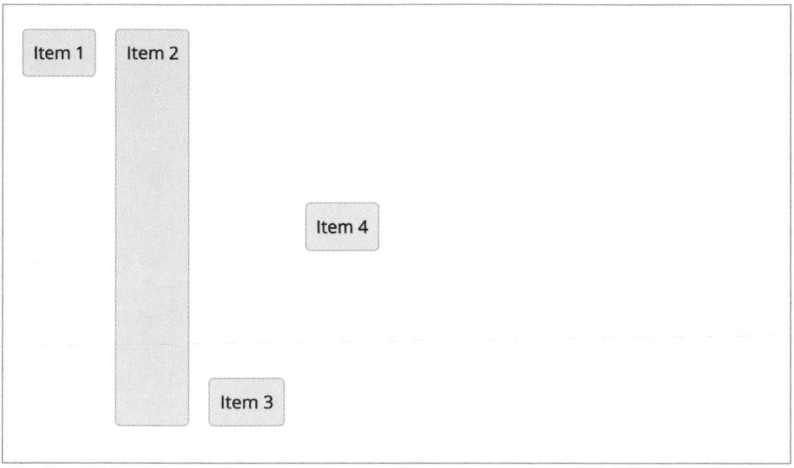

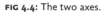

FIG 4.3: The `align-self` property sets the alignment on individual items.

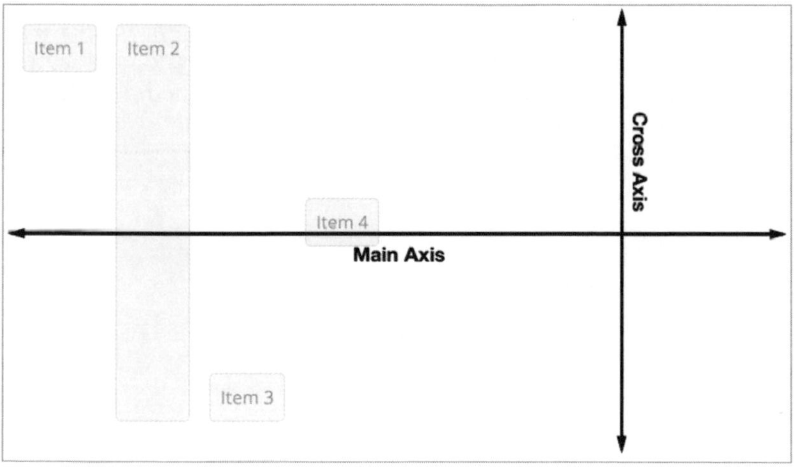

FIG 4.4: The two axes.

If we change the flex-direction to column, the cross axis becomes horizontal. Aligning our items to flex-end moves the column over to the right-hand side (**FIG 4.5**).

```
.cards {
  display: flex;
  flex-direction: column;
  align-items: flex-end;
}
```

Code example: http://bkaprt.com/ncl/04-04/

ALIGNING GRID ITEMS

If you know how to align items in flexbox, you'll find that it works the same way for Grid.

To demonstrate alignment in CSS Grid Layout, this time I create a four-column and three-row track grid, and lay my items out on the grid using the named areas method I showed you in Chapter 3.

```
.cards {
  display: grid;
  grid-template-columns: repeat(4, 1fr);
  grid-template-rows: repeat(3, 100px);
  grid-template-areas:
    "a a a b"
    "a a a b"
    "c d d d";
  grid-gap: 20px;
}
  .one { grid-area: a; }
  .two {  grid-area: b; }
  .three { grid-area: c; }
  .four { grid-area: d; }
```

Code example: http://bkaprt.com/ncl/04-05/

FIG 4.5: The items displayed as a column align to the end of the flex container.

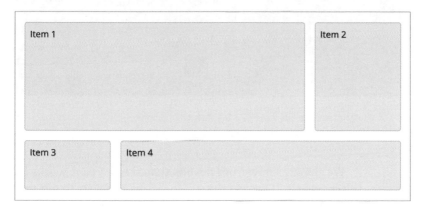

FIG 4.6: A four-column, three-row grid with four grid areas.

The default value for align-items is stretch, just like in flexbox. So if we load this example in a browser, we can see the grid areas we've defined (FIG 4.6).

A quick tip: as we start to look at more complex examples, it helps to see the grid defined. Firefox DevTools has a grid highlighter tool (http://bkaprt.com/ncl/04-06/). Inspect the element, then click the little grid icon to see your grid (FIG 4.7).

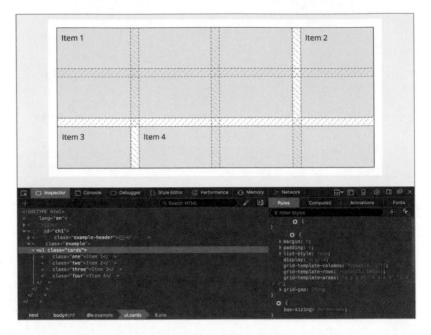

FIG 4.7: Our grid, with the lines and gaps highlighted in Firefox.

We already know from flexbox that `align-items` works on the cross axis. If we add the `align-items` property to our grid container with a value of `start`, the items all line up at the top of their area (**FIG 4.8**).

```
.cards {
  display: grid;
  grid-template-columns: repeat(4, 1fr);
  grid-template-rows: repeat(3, 100px);
  grid-template-areas:
    "a a a b"
    "a a a b"
    "c d d d";
  grid-gap: 20px;
  align-items: start;
}
```

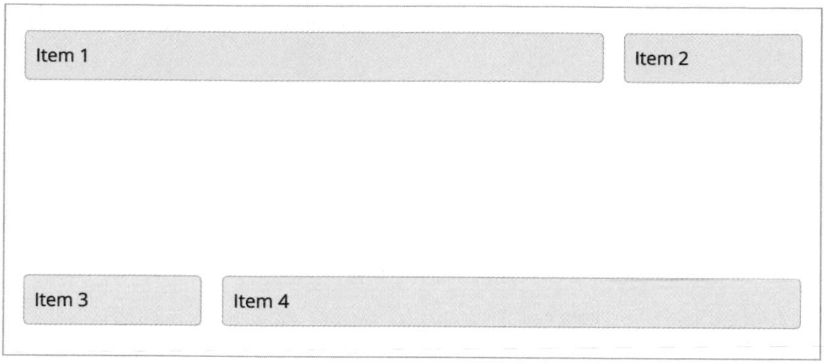

FIG 4.8: The grid with `align-items` set to `start`.

The background on the area no longer extends to the end of the grid area; instead, it comes up to sit behind the content.

As we did with flexbox, we can use the `align-self` property to override alignment on individual items.

```
.two {
  grid-area: b;
  align-self: stretch;
}
.three {
  grid-area: c;
  align-self: flex-end;
}
.four {
  grid-area: d;
  align-self: center;
}
```

Code example: http://bkaprt.com/ncl/04-07/

This aligns the items inside their grid area on the block (or column) axis.

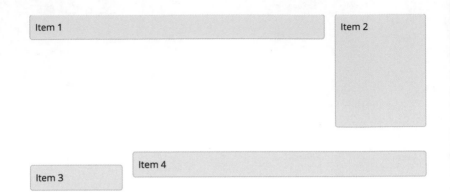

FIG 4.9: The grid items aligning to start, stretch, end, and center of their grid area.

JUSTIFYING GRID ITEMS

We can also perform alignment of grid items along the row (or inline) axis with the `justify-items` property, which sets the `justify-self` value of the individual grid items.

The initial value of `justify-items` in Grid Layout is `stretch`, so the items stretch over their entire area. If we set the value to `end`, the items shift over to the end of their area—to the right when working in a left-to-right language (**FIG 4.10**).

```
.cards {
  display: grid;
  grid-template-columns: repeat(4, 1fr);
  grid-template-rows: repeat(3, 100px);
  grid-template-areas:
    "a a a b"
    "a a a b"
    "c d d d";
  grid-gap: 20px;
  justify-items: end;
}
```

Code example: http://bkaprt.com/ncl/04-08/

FIG 4.10: The items all move to the end-column line of their area.

You can also use the `justify-self` property with the same values as for `justify-items` to target an individual grid item:

```
.four {
  grid-area: d;
  justify-self: stretch;
}
```

JUSTIFYING FLEX ITEMS

The `justify-items` and `justify-self` properties do not apply in flexbox because we only have one axis, and the main axis might have multiple items on it. There may be times, however, when we want to space items out on the main axis; to do so, we need to space out the content itself. For this, we use the `justify-content` property, which affects the entire flex container. The `justify-content` property acts on the main axis—on the row if our `flex-direction` is row, on the column if `flex-direction` is `column`.

The initial value of `justify-content` is `flex-start`. That's why, when you declare `display: flex` on the parent, if you do nothing else, your items will line up at the start of the flex

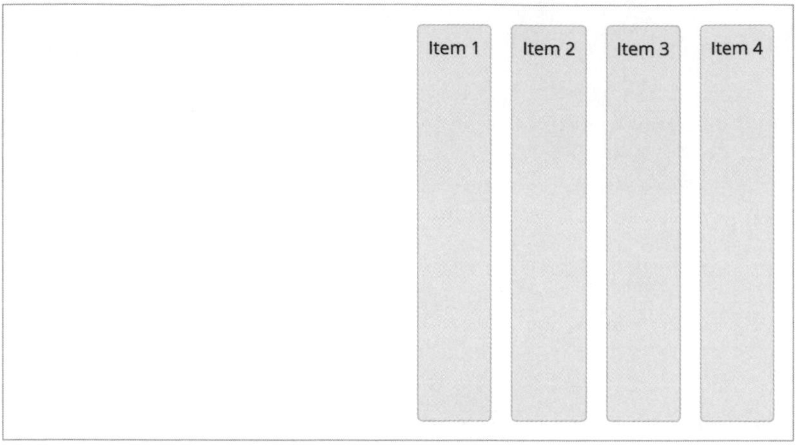

FIG 4.11: These flex items are set to `justify-content: flex-end`.

container—the left-hand side in a left-to-right language. If you set it to flex-end, your items will line up at the end (**FIG 4.11**).

```
.cards {
  display: flex;
  justify-content: flex-end;
}
```

Code example: http://bkaprt.com/ncl/04-09/

Making space around and between items

The justify-content property is also the property used to space items out along the main axis. The value space-between creates an equal amount of space between our items; space-around creates an equal amount of space around the items. A third value, space-evenly, distributes the items evenly on the main axis.

The simplest way to center a box

You can use `align-items` and `justify-content` on the same flex item, which makes it easy to properly center an element. We can place our item into a container, set that container to `display: flex`, and set `align-items` and `justify-content` to `center`.

```
.example {
  height: 50vh;
  display: flex;
  justify-content: center;
  align-items: center;
}
```

Code example: http://bkaprt.com/ncl/04-10/

It may seem like overkill to make something a flex item just to center it—and someday we may not need to. The Box Alignment specification details how these alignment properties should work with other layout methods. In the future, we may be able to apply them no matter which layout method our content uses.

The align-content property in flexbox

The `align-content` property works on the cross axis in flexbox, which will only have free space available if the following conditions are met:

- `flex-wrap` is `wrap`
- the container is taller than the space needed to display the items

If both of these things are true, you can use `align-content` in the same way as `justify content`.

In this example, the initial value is `stretch`, so the items take up the available space in the flex container as they wrap (**FIG 4.12**).

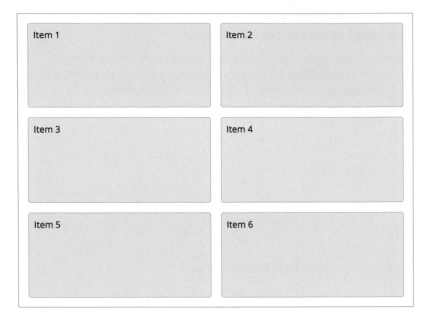

FIG 4.12: The cards wrap and take up the space in the 50vh container.

```
.cards {
  display: flex;
  flex-wrap: wrap;
  height: 50vh;
}
.cards li {
  flex: 1 1 250px;
}
```

Code example: http://bkaprt.com/ncl/04-11/

By adding the align-content property with a value of space-between, the items take as much space as they need for their content; then, the remaining space is distributed between the items. This works in the same way as justify-content on the main axis (**FIG 4.13**).

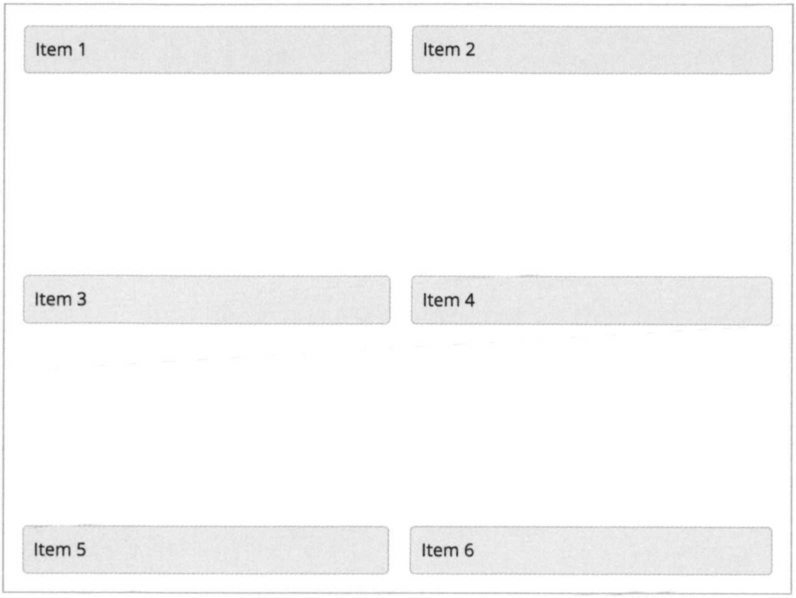

Item 1	Item 2
Item 3	Item 4
Item 5	Item 6

FIG 4.13: The items now take as much space as they need for their content; the rest of the space is distributed equally.

```
.cards {
  display: flex;
  flex-wrap: wrap;
  align-content: space-between;
  height: 50vh;
}
```

ALIGNING AND JUSTIFYING GRID TRACKS

The align-content and justify-content properties affect the grid tracks in Grid Layout. As with align-content in flexbox, you need additional space in the grid container for these to work. You would have extra space in the container if you were using fixed-sized tracks—rather than the fr unit—and these

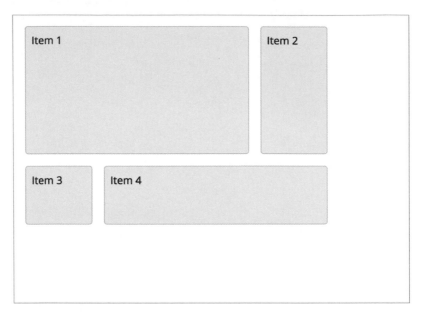

FIG 4.14: Because the initial value of align-content and justify-content is start, the tracks sit at the top left of the container.

tracks added up in total to a smaller height or width than that set on your grid container.

In my next example, I've created grid tracks that are smaller than the total size of the grid container in both dimensions (**FIG 4.14**).

Adding the align-content and justify-content properties with a value of space-between spaces out the tracks in both dimensions (**FIG 4.15**).

```
.cards {
  display: grid;
  grid-template-columns: repeat(4, 15%);
  grid-template-rows: repeat(3, 100px);
  height: 50vh;
```

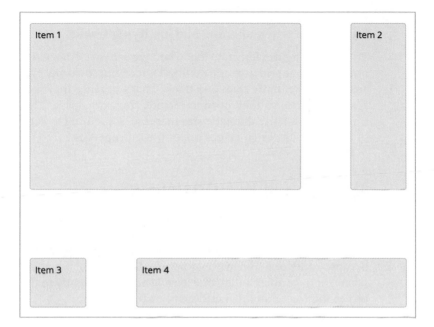

FIG 4.15: After adding `align-content` and `justify-content`.

```
grid-template-areas:
            "a a a b"
            "a a a b"
            "c d d d";
grid-gap: 20px;
align-content: space-between;
justify-content: space-between;
}
```

Code example: http://bkaprt.com/ncl/04-12/

Extra space when aligning and justifying tracks

The last two figures illustrate that when we use `space-between`, not only do our grid gaps appear to get wider, but so do any grid areas that span more than one track. That's because they also span over gaps, so they need to include the extra space. This can result in a fairly dramatic size increase, something to keep in mind if your design makes use of these properties.

ALIGNMENT WITH AUTO MARGINS

It can be helpful, particularly with flexbox, to use the fact that auto margins play very nicely with these alignment values.

We've already seen that `justify-items` is not part of flexbox because of its one-dimensional nature. Sometimes, however, you want to be able to align one item in a row differently to the rest of the row. Enter the auto-margins trick!

If you've ever centered a block by setting the right and left margins to `auto`, you know that auto margins absorb any available space. By setting both at once, we have two margins that both want all the space, so the block ends up in the middle. We can apply that to a list of flex items. In the following example, I have a set of flex items displayed per the initial values of flexbox lined up on the left. If I give `last-child` a left margin of `auto`, that margin takes up all the space and pushes that one item over to the right (**FIG 4.16**).

```
.cards {
  display: flex;
}
.cards li:last-child {
  margin-left: auto;
}
```

Code example: http://bkaprt.com/ncl/04-13/

| Item 1 | Item 2 | Item 3 | | Item 4 |

FIG 4.16: By using the auto-margins trick, we can align one flex item to the right.

LOGICAL VS. PHYSICAL PROPERTIES

In all of this alignment discussion, it may have occurred to you to wonder why we talk about "start" and "end" of Grid and flex containers, rather than just referring to left, right, top, and bottom, as we do in absolute positioning.

The left, right, top, and bottom properties used as offsets in absolute positioning are known as *physical* properties: they explain where something is physically located on the screen. In layout, however, the writing mode of the document matters, so with newer layout methods we use *logical* properties to describe the start edge of our container—wherever that is in terms of the writing mode we are currently in.

We can see a simple illustration of the difference between logical and physical properties and values by taking the last example—auto margins—and adding an rtl value to the dir attribute on the body element.

```
<html lang="en" dir="rtl">
```

Here, flexbox uses the logical value of flex-start as the initial value, and arranges the items from that starting point. We used a physical value of margin-left to assign our auto-margin. This now doesn't work—we would need to go into our CSS and update that to margin-right to get the same effect.

A specification is currently in development that will map logical properties to all of the physical properties we are accustomed to using in CSS (http://bkaprt.com/ncl/04-14/). This should make designing for multiple writing modes easier in the future. For now, if you need to support multiple writing modes with one design, be mindful of where physical properties are used and account for those yourself.

FIG 4.17: The flexbox navigation menu now starts on the right; Item 1 is the farthest to the right.

The more I work with flexbox and Grid Layout, the more I find that an understanding of alignment is key to leveraging the power of these specifications. It's also a domain we're very unused to having such control over—so don't worry if at first you constantly have to look up which axis is which, or remind yourself whether you are aligning content or items this time. In Chapter 5, we'll explore one area in which this control of alignment is necessary: creating flexible grids and responsive layouts.

RESPONSIVE BY DEFAULT

WHEN CREATING A RESPONSIVE design, being able to align items individually and as a group is important. We can't work in absolute values, lining things up relative to a fixed point on a screen, if we have no fixed point to work from. Alignment is just one way in which we see how these modern methods of layout are responsive by default, designed for a world of flexible grids. In this chapter, we'll look at those flexible grids, and think about how to make the most of the functionality in the specification.

In Chapter 1, we looked at a simple example of creating a layout using floats that had a flexible grid. To do this, we need to calculate the width of our floated column as a percentage of the available width, making sure to account for any margins between columns. We also need to employ media queries to change the number of columns, or to cause blocks to span more columns as the viewport size decreases. We can end up with a fair amount of CSS for each layout just to cope with this rearrangement of items at different breakpoints.

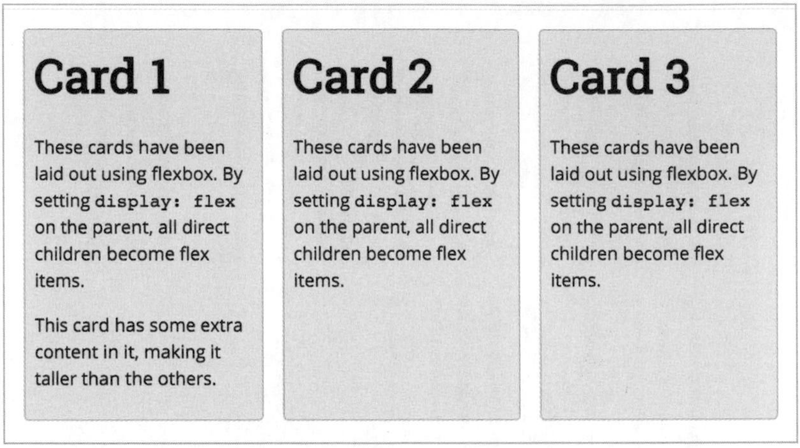

Card 1

These cards have been laid out using flexbox. By setting `display: flex` on the parent, all direct children become flex items.

This card has some extra content in it, making it taller than the others.

Card 2

These cards have been laid out using flexbox. By setting `display: flex` on the parent, all direct children become flex items.

Card 3

These cards have been laid out using flexbox. By setting `display: flex` on the parent, all direct children become flex items.

FIG 5.1: Three equal-width flex items.

In flexbox, however, we can easily have three equal-width columns (**FIG 5.1**):

```
.cards {
  display: flex;
}
.cards li {
  flex: 1;
}
```

Code example: http://bkaprt.com/ncl/05-01/

We can also allow the container width to dictate how many items will display in each row—without the need of a media query or breakpoint (**FIG 5.2**).

Because we explored the difference between flexbox and Grid in Chapter 3, you understand that the reason the cards on Row 2 don't line up in a grid formation is because flexbox is one-dimensional. To create a strict grid, we can switch to Grid Layout.

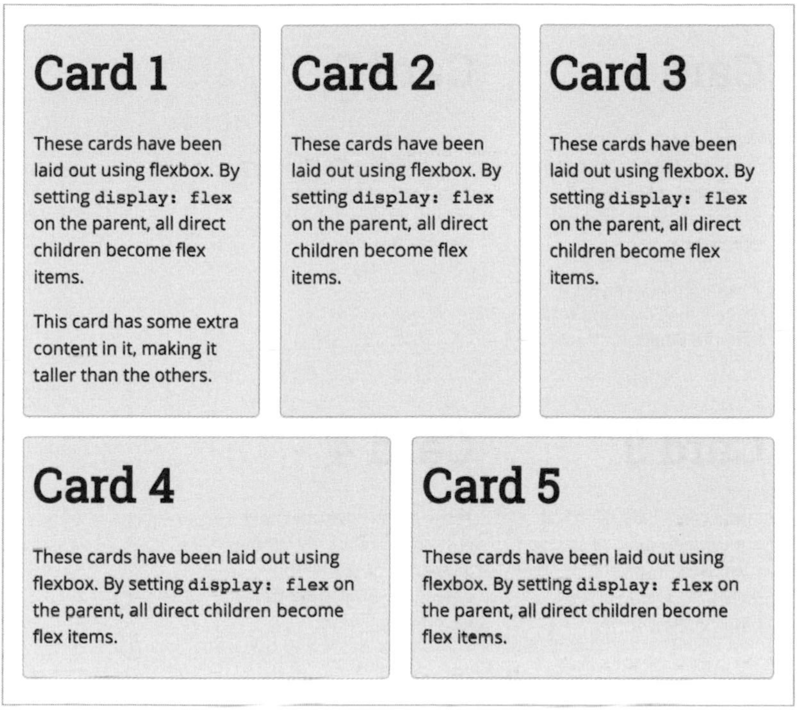

FIG 5.2: Wrapped flex items.

```
.cards {
  display: grid;
  grid-template-columns: repeat(3, 1fr);
}
```

Note that these two examples differ. In the flexbox example, if we have more available space, the items will accumulate incrementally in one row before wrapping. If space decreases, we'll eventually drop down to a single item per row.

We can achieve similar results with Grid Layout; doing so reminds us that Grid works from the outside in. *We define a grid, and then put items into it.*

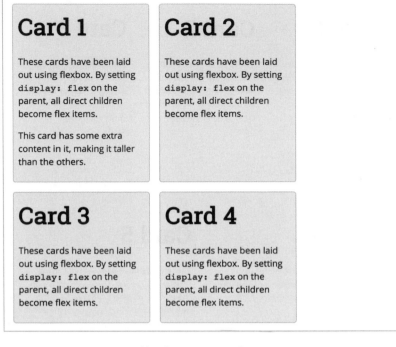

Card 1

These cards have been laid out using flexbox. By setting `display: flex` on the parent, all direct children become flex items.

This card has some extra content in it, making it taller than the others.

Card 2

These cards have been laid out using flexbox. By setting `display: flex` on the parent, all direct children become flex items.

Card 3

These cards have been laid out using flexbox. By setting `display: flex` on the parent, all direct children become flex items.

Card 4

These cards have been laid out using flexbox. By setting `display: flex` on the parent, all direct children become flex items.

FIG 5.3: At narrower screen widths, the rows contain fewer items.

To make a grid with a flexible number of columns, we need to create the column listing on the grid container itself; we need to instruct it to "add as many column tracks as will fit." With that in mind, let's take another look at the repeat() notation used in the earlier examples. Our current grid always has three tracks; I've used repeat() notation to create my track listing, and requested three column tracks each of 1fr.

What I want to do is to say "as many as will fit" rather than 3, as the first value of repeat(). So instead of using the integer 3, I use the keyword auto-fill (**FIG 5.4**). For the column-track width, I then need to use an absolute value; if we used 1fr, we would only get one column track, since 1fr would use all the available space in the grid container.

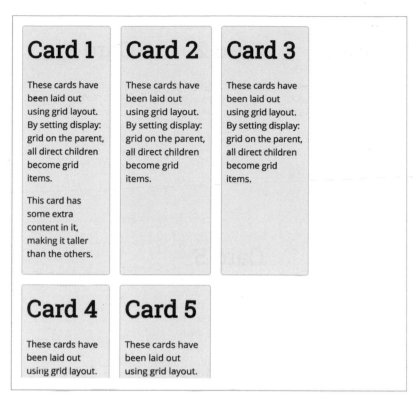

Card 1

These cards have been laid out using grid layout. By setting display: grid on the parent, all direct children become grid items.

This card has some extra content in it, making it taller than the others.

Card 2

These cards have been laid out using grid layout. By setting display: grid on the parent, all direct children become grid items.

Card 3

These cards have been laid out using grid layout. By setting display: grid on the parent, all direct children become grid items.

Card 4

These cards have been laid out using grid layout.

Card 5

These cards have been laid out using grid layout.

FIG 5.4: As many 200-pixel column tracks as will fit into the container.

```
.cards {
  display: grid;
  grid-template-columns: repeat(auto-fill, 200px);
}
```

Code example: http://bkaprt.com/ncl/05-02/

If you drag the window wider and smaller, you can see that the browser creates as many 200-pixel column tracks as it can in the grid container. This isn't quite the same as flexbox, however, since we now have fixed track sizes. If the container doesn't divide neatly by 200 pixels, we get a gap at the end.

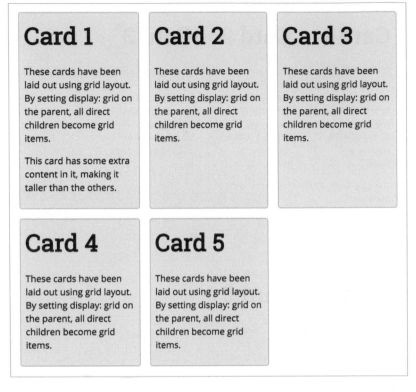

FIG 5.5: As many 200-pixels tracks as will fit, with the additional space distributed evenly.

To address this, we can employ another trick, with the `min-max()` function. Using `minmax()` in track sizing enables the setting of a minimum and a maximum size for that track. If we update the 200-pixel track definition to `minmax(200px, 1fr)`, the browser will work out how many 200-pixel columns will fit into the container, and then take the leftover space and assign it equally to the tracks, since the maximum is `1fr`.

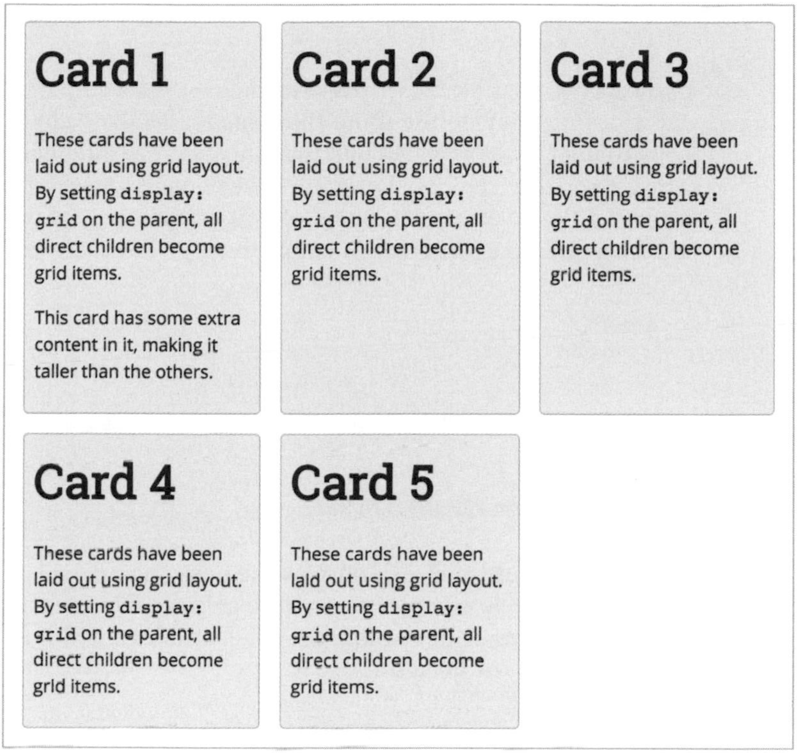

Card 1	Card 2	Card 3
These cards have been laid out using grid layout. By setting `display: grid` on the parent, all direct children become grid items. This card has some extra content in it, making it taller than the others.	These cards have been laid out using grid layout. By setting `display: grid` on the parent, all direct children become grid items.	These cards have been laid out using grid layout. By setting `display: grid` on the parent, all direct children become grid items.
Card 4	Card 5	
These cards have been laid out using grid layout. By setting `display: grid` on the parent, all direct children become grid items.	These cards have been laid out using grid layout. By setting `display: grid` on the parent, all direct children become grid items.	

FIG 5.6: With auto-fill, the space for empty tracks is reserved.

```
.cards {
  display: grid;
  grid-template-columns: repeat(auto-fill,
  minmax(200px,1fr));
}
```

Code example: http://bkaprt.com/ncl/05-03/

We now have as many tracks as will fit in the container. The tracks have a flexible width, but won't collapse below a minimum, and the layout remains a strict grid.

auto-fill VS. auto-fit

There are two possible keywords to use in `repeat()`: `auto-fill` and `auto-fit`. They do the same thing insofar as they add as many column tracks as will fit into the container. The difference is that if you use `auto-fill` but don't have enough items to fill the tracks, the tracks remain open, so you will get space at the end where the reserved column tracks are.

```
.cards {
  display: grid;
  grid-template-columns: repeat(auto-fill,
  minmax(100px, 1fr));
}
```

Code example: http://bkaprt.com/ncl/05-04/

If we instead use `auto-fit`, once all the items have been laid out, any completely empty tracks will be collapsed. In the case of a flexible listing such as ours, the available space will then be distributed to the filled tracks (**FIG 5.7**).

```
.cards {
  display: grid;
  grid-template-columns: repeat(auto-fit,
  minmax(100px, 1fr));
}
```

Use `auto-fill` if you want to maintain the tracks; use `auto-fit` if you want the content to fill the container (in case there are fewer items than tracks).

The ability to maintain proportions is a key requirement for responsive designs, and our new layout methods enable this. We briefly met the methods for creating flexibly sized items and grid tracks in previous chapters; now it's time to fully understand how they work. The key to flexible sizing in flexbox lies in three properties: `flex-grow`, `flex-shrink`, and `flex-basis`. These are applied to the flex items. In Grid, we have the `fr` unit, which is used when creating track sizes.

FIG 5.7: With auto-fit, the tracks are collapsed. If we are distributing space with a max of 1fr, the leftover space is reassigned.

CONTROLLING SIZING WITH THE flex PROPERTIES

To control the sizing of flex items, we need to add rules to the flex items themselves, and we do this by using three properties:

flex-grow
flex-shrink
flex-basis

The flex-basis property can be used to set a width (if flex-direction is row) or height (if flex-direction is column) for the flex item. If you give all items a flex-basis of 200 pixels, the browser will assign 200 pixels of space to each item.

The flex-grow property defines whether an item can grow larger than the size set in flex-basis. If you set flex-grow to 1, you allow items to grow larger than 200 pixels in order to take up any free space in the flex container.

The flex-shrink property determines whether an item can shrink smaller than the flex-basis value. If you have a non-wrapping 500-pixel-width container and three items with a flex-basis of 200 pixels, they will overflow unless flex-shrink is greater than 0.

The flex shorthand

The specification advises that authors use the flex shorthand rather than the individual properties of flex-grow, flex-shrink, and flex-basis (http://bkaprt.com/ncl/05-05/). Given their interaction with one another, it's certainly easier to see what you're doing if you treat these three values as one property. Therefore, my examples all use the flex property rather than the individual components; the order of the values is as follows:

```
flex-grow
flex-shrink
flex-basis
```

In this first example, I have three flex items. They all have a flex-grow value of 0, flex-shrink of 0, and flex-basis of 200px (**FIG 5.8**). Therefore, they do not grow to fill the flex container; if it becomes smaller than the total size needed to display the items, they'll overflow.

```
.cards li {
  flex: 0 0 200px;
}
```

If I change flex-grow to 1, the items now stretch equally to fill the container (**FIG 5.9**).

```
.cards li {
  flex: 1 0 200px;
}
```

If I target the first item and change flex-grow on just that item to 2, it grows more than the other two items (**FIG 5.10**). In this way, the flex properties allow you to scale items in proportion to one another.

```
.cards li {
  flex: 1 0 200px;
}
```

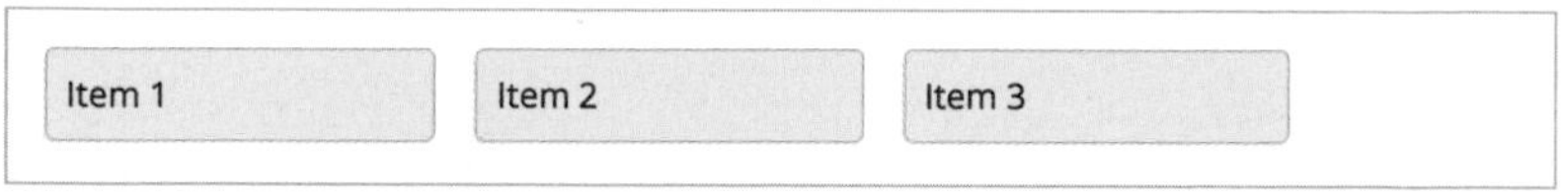

FIG 5.8: The items display at 200 pixels wide.

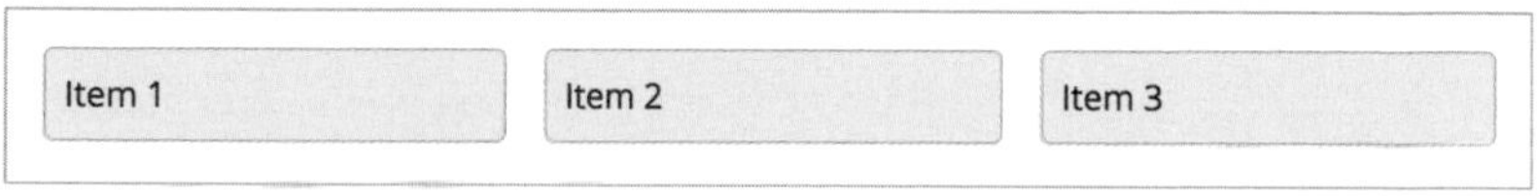

FIG 5.9: The items can now grow wider than 200 pixels.

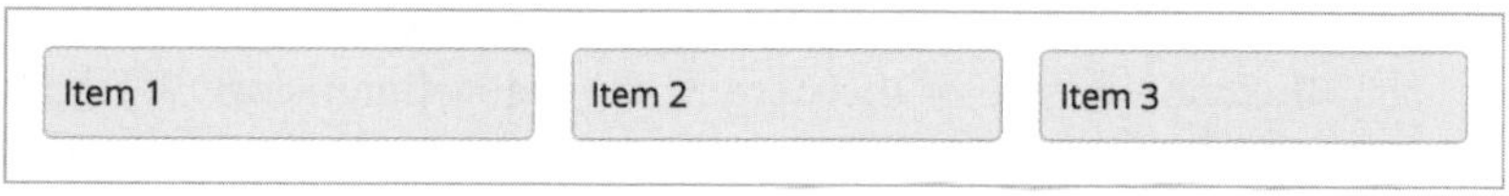

FIG 5.10: The first item now has a flex-grow factor of 2 and gets twice as much of the leftover space.

FIG 5.11: Set flex-grow to 0 for equal distribution of all the available space.

```
.cards li:first-child {
  flex: 2 0 200px;
}
```

Code example: http://bkaprt.com/ncl/05-06/

Note that Item 1 has now increased to twice the size of the other two items. Our flex-basis value is 200 pixels, which means that the browser first accounts for 3 × 200 pixels, and then, with the remaining space, distributes it per the flex-grow factor. The increase in size can therefore be quite subtle. If you want space to be distributed evenly, set flex-basis to 0 (**FIG 5.11**).

```
.cards li {
  flex: 1 0 0;
}

.cards li:first-child {
  flex: 2 0 0;
}
```

The content and auto keywords for flex-basis

In addition to accepting a length unit, flex-basis can take the keyword values of content and auto.

A value of content means that the flex-basis is taken from the content size of the item in the main dimension. Working with flex-direction set to row, the main dimension is the row, so flexbox will look at the width of the item and use that in the same way it uses a length unit you specify.

Then we have the very useful value of auto. Use auto as your flex-basis and, if you've set a width on the item, that width will be used as the flex-basis value. If you haven't set a width, auto resolves to the content size.

In this example, I have three items and have set the flex-basis to auto (**FIG 5.12**). I've then given an absolute width to the third item, with the width property. Flexbox is now using that width as the flex-basis for the third item; the other two use the content width.

```
.cards li {
  flex: 1 1 auto;
}
.cards li:last-child {
  width: 400px;
}
```

Code example: http://bkaprt.com/ncl/05-07/

FIG 5.12: The `width` on the last item is used as the `flex-basis` value.

FIG 5.13: The `fr` unit layout. The column tracks grow and shrink proportionally.

I would suggest using `auto` as your starting point for `flex-basis` unless you know that you have a specific requirement. Doing so means that by setting a `width` on your item, or by way of the content requiring a certain amount of space, things will often work out well. But there is much value in playing with and testing exactly how the flex properties work; the things that flexbox does that seem mysterious are very much tied up in them.

Keeping things in proportion in Grid Layout with fr units

In CSS Grid Layout, we generally define our proportions when we define our tracks, rather than work from the content out. For this we have the `fr` unit, which we've already met. So far, we have only seen the `fr` unit in action creating equal-width tracks, but it can also be used much like `flex-grow` to define a portion of the available space.

In my next example, I've created a layout with three tracks; the sidebars are `1fr` each and the middle track is `4fr`. The available space in the grid container is divided into six: one part given to each of the `1fr` tracks, and four parts to the `4fr` track (**FIG 5.13**).

```
.example {
    display: grid;
    grid-template-columns: 1fr 4fr 1fr;
    grid-gap: 20px;
}
.content {
    grid-column: 2;
}
.sidebar1 {
    grid-column: 1;
    grid-row: 1;
}
.sidebar2 {
    grid-column: 3;
    grid-row: 1;
}
```

Code example: http://bkaprt.com/ncl/05-08/

The nice thing about fraction units is that, because they define a fraction of the available space, they can be mixed with tracks set using absolute units.

In the next example, I've changed my track listing to create a layout that used to be referred to as the "Holy Grail." The Holy Grail layout describes fixed-width sidebars and a stretchy middle, with the main content area coming first in the source (**FIG 5.14**). The middle track is 1fr, so it takes up all available space after the fixed sidebar, and any grid-gap has been accounted for.

```
.example {
    display: grid;
    grid-template-columns: 150px 1fr 150px;
    grid-gap: 20px;
}
```

| Sidebar 1: 150px | Main content: 1fr | Sidebar 2: 150px |

FIG 5.14: The "Holy Grail" layout.

The behavior of auto in Grid Layout

In the section about flex-basis, I described how auto works in flexbox, taking the width of the item or resolving to content. In Grid Layout, auto works in roughly the same way; however, be aware that it affects the entire row or column track.

In this example, the middle column track is set to auto, and since we have not set a track size for rows, the auto-generated rows will also be auto-sized. The item card2 appears in the middle track and, as the widest item in that track, causes the entire track to take 300 pixels. The item card4 is on the second row and forces the entire row track to 300 pixels tall (FIG 5.15).

```
.cards {
  display: grid;
  grid-gap: 20px;
  grid-template-columns: 1fr auto 1fr;
}
.cards .card2 {
  width: 300px;
}
.cards .card4 {
  height: 300px;
}
```

Code example: http://bkaprt.com/ncl/05-09/

Although allowing rows to auto-size is generally desirable, in some cases, setting columns to auto may result in strange sizing if something in the track affects the widths. Something to keep in mind!

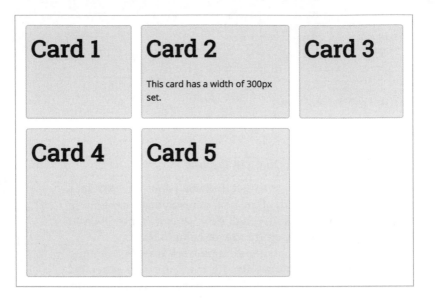

FIG 5.15: Auto-sized row tracks may have their size affected by items, or by the content of items.

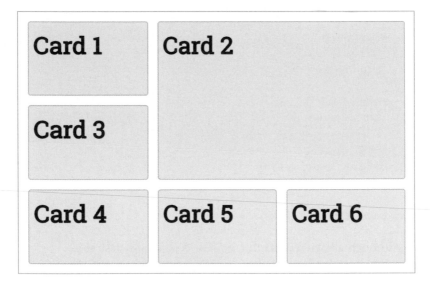

FIG 5.16: A neat grid with 150-pixel-tall tracks.

Using auto as a maximum in minmax()

Because auto can generally be expected to mean "content-sized," it can be usefully employed as the maximum in minmax(). This enables the creation of tracks that are always a minimum height or width, but that expand if more content is added than expected.

In this example, I've created a very neat set of boxes. Each row track is a minimum of 150 pixels tall; If an area spans two rows, it becomes 320 pixels tall, including the grid-gap of 20px. The item card2 is an example of this (**FIG 5.16**).

```css
.cards {
  display: grid;
  grid-gap: 20px;
  grid-template-columns: 1fr 1fr 1fr;
  grid-auto-rows: minmax(150px, auto);
}
.card1 {
  grid-column: 1;
  grid-row: 1;
}
.card2 {
  grid-column: 2 / 4;
  grid-row: 1 / 3;
}
```

Code example: http://bkaprt.com/ncl/05-10/

The track sizing is achieved using the minmax() function we met earlier, with our minimum set to the ideal size of the track—150px—and our maximum set to auto. This means that as long as the content is shorter than 150px, we get a 150-pixel track, as designed.

And if someone comes along and adds additional text into any box, the design adapts: the full row extends down to contain the content. The item card2 is now also taller, as the full row track 1 has expanded (**FIG 5.17**).

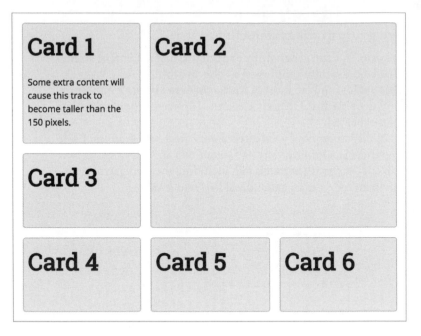

FIG 5.17: Row 1 expands to contain the content.

As you can see from this small example, Grid enables the creation of very neat, precise layouts that accommodate the real world of content on the web and the variety of devices we need to support. The ability to easily place items anywhere on a grid is powerful and will make existing layouts easier, and enable new design on the web. However, it brings with it a whole new range of potential accessibility issues. We'll look at those next.

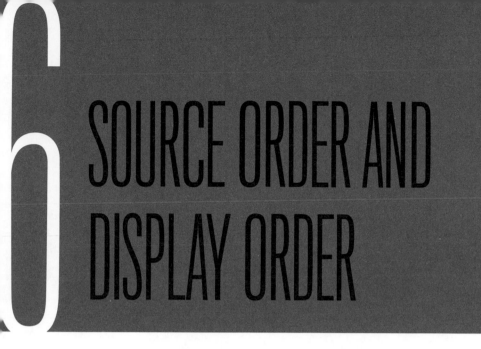

SOURCE ORDER AND DISPLAY ORDER

THE HOLY GRAIL layout in Chapter 5 illustrated something important about our new layout methods: they enable the visual display of page elements in an order other than that described in the source. This was previously only possible by taking an item out of flow with absolute positioning—something that turned out not to be all that useful for layout. This ability to disconnect visual display and source order can be used for good and bad alike; we'll look at the benefits (and risks) in this chapter.

DIRECTION OF FLOW IN FLEXBOX

The default behavior of flex items is to lay themselves out in document order—the order in which they appear in the source. The flexbox specification includes the property flex-direction, which is how we choose whether to display items as a row or as a column. This property can also be used to change the direction in which the flex items lay themselves out.

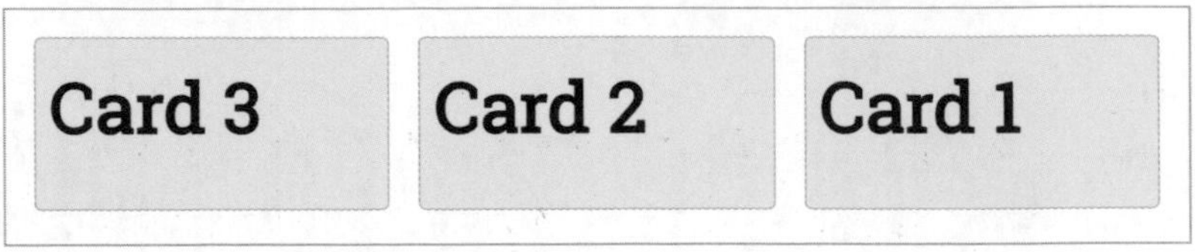

FIG 6.1: The items display in reverse order.

The following cards display one after the other in the order in which they appear in the source. If I set flex-direction to row-reverse, they flip and start to display from the end of the flex container (FIG 6.1).

```
.cards {
  display: flex;
  flex-direction: row-reverse;
}
```

Code example: http://bkaprt.com/ncl/06-01/

Similarly, if flex-direction is column, you can also choose column-reverse (FIG 6.2).

```
.cards {
  display: flex;
  flex-direction: column-reverse;
}
```

The flex-direction values relate to writing modes. In a right-to-left language, row-reverse would cause the text to start from the left-hand side of the flex container.

FIG 6.2: The items display in reverse order as a column.

DIRECTION OF FLOW IN GRID LAYOUT

If you are explicitly placing items on your grid—either by using line-based placement or template areas—you can avoid Grid auto-placing any items for you. We've already seen examples of Grid auto-placement, though. As soon as you create a grid, any direct child flows into that grid—one item per cell. These auto-placement rules can be used in various ways to change the way content flows into the grid.

Where Grid is most like flexbox is in the `grid-auto-flow` property. By default, this property is set to `row`. Therefore, when working in a left-to-right language, items start at the top left of the grid container and position themselves into cells working to the right, then move on to the next row. Grid will create new rows in the implicit grid as required for the items it needs to place.

You can instead give `grid-auto-flow` a value of `column`. In this case, Grid will display the items as a column, filling the available rows and creating new columns in the implicit grid as required (**FIG 6.3**).

FIG 6.3: A two-row track grid, with content displayed with `grid-auto-flow: column`.

```
.cards {
  display: grid;
  grid-auto-flow: column;
  grid-template-rows: repeat(2,auto);
}
```

Code example: http://bkaprt.com/ncl/06-02/

As with `flex-direction` in flexbox, these values are writing-mode-aware.

GRID AUTO-PLACEMENT

The auto-placement rules in Grid do not stop at enabling the flow direction of grid items. Working with Grid auto-placement can almost feel like a completely different layout model again, if your first impression of Grid is a method to define a grid and then state where you want elements to be placed on it. Many common UI tasks can be achieved with the use of auto-placement, and understanding how it behaves is key to reducing the amount of Grid code you need to write.

Let's start by playing with the number of tracks auto-placed items can span. The next example is a set of cards, some of which display in portrait mode and others in landscape.

We can lay these out using auto-placement by adding rules to the landscape items, causing them to start on line auto, but end on line span 2 (**FIG 6.4**). So auto-placement will decide where to put them, but they will always span two tracks.

```
.cards {
    display: grid;
    grid-template-columns: repeat(auto-fill,
  minmax(250px, 1fr));

}
.cards .landscape {
    grid-column: auto / span 2;
}
```

Code example: http://bkaprt.com/ncl/06-03/

Here, items stay in document source order. When Grid encounters an item that doesn't fit, it leaves a gap and moves on to the next row. It's possible to backfill those gaps, however.

We met the grid-auto-flow property earlier in this chapter, when we used it to set the direction of auto-placement to column. This property can also take a keyword of dense or sparse, with sparse the default.

```
.cards {
    display: grid;
    grid-template-columns: repeat(auto-fill,
  minmax(250px, 1fr));
    grid-auto-flow: dense;
}
```

If we now look at our example, rather than a gap being left, Card 4 has been moved out of document source order to fill the gap between the second and third cards. Card 6 then appears between Card 3 and Card 5. We end up with a neat grid with no gaps; however, the items are now visually displayed in a different order from the way they are listed in the document source (**FIG 6.5**).

Card 1

I am a portrait format card. I will display in a single grid column track.

Card 2

I am a portrait format card. I will display in a single grid column track.

Card 3

I am a landscape format card. I will display across two grid column tracks.

Card 4

I am a portrait format card. I will display in a single grid column track.

Card 5

I am a landscape format card. I will display across two grid column tracks.

Card 6

I am a portrait format card. I will display in a single grid column track.

Card 7

I am a portrait format card. I will display in a single grid column track.

FIG 6.4: The items span one column track by default. With a class of .landscape, they span two.

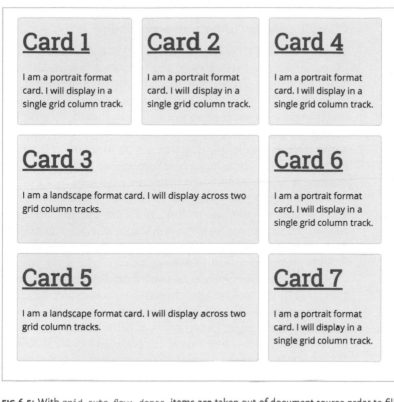

FIG 6.5: With `grid-auto-flow: dense`, items are taken out of document source order to fill the gaps.

This behavior can be very handy if you have a collection of elements that lack a logical order. That may be the case for a photo gallery, for example; the images may not need to be displayed in any particular order on the page. Even then, though, you need to take care; with the power of reordering also comes a responsibility to use this feature sensibly, not causing the layout to become burdensome for someone who doesn't use the web like many of us do.

Changing display order and accessibility

The flexbox and Grid specifications both deal with the issue of accessibility and reordering, and both state that visual reordering does not change the logical order of the document. In practice, this means that the default tab order, for someone navigating around your site with a keyboard, follows the source and not the display. If you reorder the display through auto-placement, or by placing items in an order other than the document order, you could cause someone to jump around the document haphazardly when using the keyboard.

You can see this in our grid-auto-flow: dense example. If you try tabbing from link to link, you'll see that the tab order follows the order in which the items appear in the source, not in the modified order you can see on screen.

This means you need to take great care whenever you do something that takes elements away from the order in which they exist in the source. You should always consider whether it makes sense also to update the source to maintain the logical order. For an excellent explanation of the problems caused by disconnecting source and visual display, read Léonie Watson's "Flexbox & the keyboard navigation disconnect" (http://bkaprt.com/ncl/06-04/).

THE order PROPERTY IN FLEXBOX AND GRID

The flexbox and Grid specifications include the order property, which can set an order for flex or Grid items.

Using the order property in flexbox changes the display order of the items.

```
.cards {
  display: flex;
}
```

```
.cards li:nth-child(1) {
  order: 3;
}
.cards li:nth-child(2) {
  order: 1;
}
.cards li:nth-child(3) {
  order: 2;
}
```

Code example: http://bkaprt.com/ncl/06-05/

You can also use the order property in Grid, although here the use seems less obvious; if you want to define a specific position for an item, one of the methods of placing items might be more appropriate. If you use order, however, it will affect auto-placement, since items are placed in what is described as "order-modified document order" (http://bkaprt.com/ncl/06-06/).

In this example, I have given one item (the very first grid item) an order value of 10. The initial value of order is 0, so all items without an order have an order of 0; since 10 is greater than 0, Item 1 should now appear at the end of the list of items. You can see that auto-placement has honored this order and placed the item last (**FIG 6.6**).

```
.cards li:nth-child(1) {
  order: 10;
}
```

Code example: http://bkaprt.com/ncl/05-06/

As with other reordering, this only changes the visual display order, not the logical order in the document. If tempted to rearrange things in this manner, always ask yourself if you should instead address the logical order by updating the document.

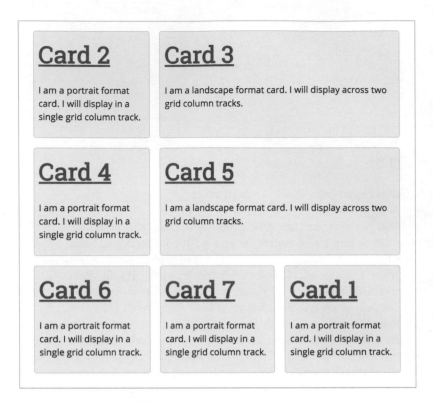

Card 2

I am a portrait format card. I will display in a single grid column track.

Card 3

I am a landscape format card. I will display across two grid column tracks.

Card 4

I am a portrait format card. I will display in a single grid column track.

Card 5

I am a landscape format card. I will display across two grid column tracks.

Card 6

I am a portrait format card. I will display in a single grid column track.

Card 7

I am a portrait format card. I will display in a single grid column track.

Card 1

I am a portrait format card. I will display in a single grid column track.

FIG 6.6: The first item is now placed last.

THE DANGER OF MARKUP "FLATTENING"

In this chapter, we've looked at some powerful features of our new layout methods—features that enable the moving of elements out of the context in which they sit in the source. This can be helpful, of course, but it represents another area where we need to consider *all* of our users, not just those who look at our design on screen, and use a mouse or trackpad to navigate.

There is a final consideration to make when developing using flexbox and Grid, and that is to avoid the temptation to flatten out markup to make it easier for elements to become flex or Grid items.

At present, an item only becomes a flex or Grid item if it is a direct child of the flex or Grid container. For example, if you create a grid for some content, then inside the content area is a list ul element—the list items inside that element will not become grid items. The ul itself could become a grid container—but it wouldn't relate to the outer grid; it would be a new nested grid. It might be tempting to decide that the list doesn't *really* need to be a list at all; if it were just a set of div elements, they would all be direct children and sit nicely on our grid. Be careful, though—*that way danger lies!*

Make good decisions for your source and then work out how to manage the visual display of items, even if that requires a little more work at the outset.

subgrid

The CSS Working Group is discussing a feature that might be a solution for this issue: subgrid, which would cascade the outer grid down to the children of a grid item, allowing our list items to participate in the same layout as their ul. While this feature was included in the Level 1 specification, it has recently been moved to Level 2. The initial spec for the feature has not yet been implemented in any browsers and the CSS Working Group felt it required extra discussion, now that people are starting to use Grid Layout. Many of us hope that this powerful feature will make its way through the discussions and be implemented very soon.

display: contents

While we wait for subgrid, a new value of the display property can give us some ability to allow indirect children to participate in our flex or Grid layouts. In the CSS Display specification, the value of contents is described thus (http://bkaprt.com/ncl/06-07/):

> *The element itself does not generate any boxes, but its children and pseudo-elements still generate boxes as normal. For the purposes of box generation and layout, the element must be*

treated as if it had been replaced with its children and pseudo-elements in the document tree.

If we take the example of a ul as described earlier, we can see how this works. In my next example, I have a grid; one of the direct children of my grid is an unordered list element. The list items inside that ul don't participate in Grid Layout, so they display one beneath the other (**FIG 6.7**).

```
.cards {
  display: grid;
  grid-gap: 20px 10px;
  grid-template-columns: repeat(auto-fill,
  minmax(200px, 1fr));
        }

.cards > * {
  background-color: #edf2ff;
  border: 1px solid #bac8ff;
  padding: 10px;
  border-radius: 5px;
}
.cards ul {
  list-style: none;
  margin: 0;
}
.cards li {
  background-color: #bac8ff;
  border:1px solid #fff;
}

<div class="cards">
  <div>
    <h2>Card 1</h2>
  </div>
  <div>
    <h2>Card 2</h2>
  </div>
```

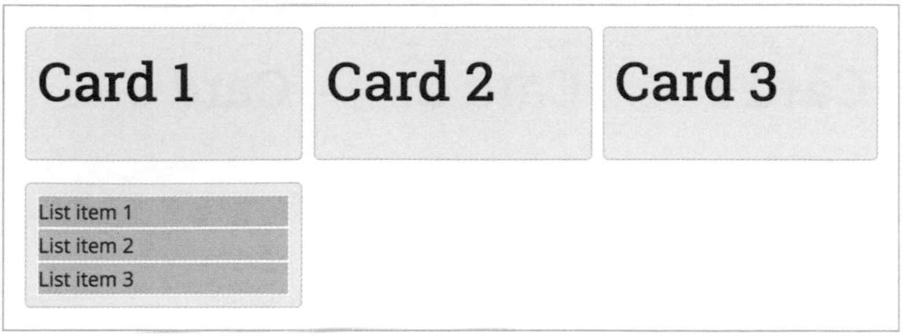

FIG 6.7: The items lay out on the grid. The subitems of the ul are not part of the grid layout.

```
<div>
   <h2>Card 3</h2>
  </div>
  <ul>
    <li>List item 1</li>
    <li>List item 2</li>
    <li>List item 3</li>
  </ul>
</div>
```

If we then add display: contents to the rules for the ul, the boxes generated by the ul disappear and the li items now lay out on the grid (**FIG 6.8**).

```
.cards ul {
  list-style: none;
  margin: 0;
  display: contents;
}
```

Code example: http://bkaprt.com/ncl/06-08/

FIG 6.8: The box for the `ul` has disappeared; the `li` elements now become part of the grid.

Note, however, that they don't take on the other styling of the direct children—only box generation is affected by `dis-play: contents`.

Judicious use of this value can help prevent markup flattening and allow you to make items deeper in the markup part of a flex or Grid layout. You probably won't want to use it everywhere, since it limits elements to being part of a very specific structure—nonetheless, it's a very useful trick to have up your sleeve.

I hope this chapter has both excited you about some of the possibilities of our new layout methods and given you food for thought about their accessibility. In Chapter 7, we'll explore how we can start to use these newer methods, given that some browsers don't yet support them.

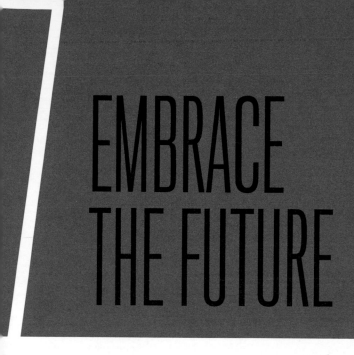

EMBRACE THE FUTURE

WEB DEVELOPERS READING about new and exciting specifications often plaintively ask, "But what about old browsers?" In this chapter, we'll survey the modern browser landscape and the ways in which CSS itself is developing methods to help us embrace new technology without leaving old browsers out in the cold.

TEST YOUR ASSUMPTIONS WITH DATA

In Chapter 2, I described how the concept of evergreen browsers is changing the way we think about browser support. Our users are increasingly likely to receive regular browser updates. Depending on the audience for the sites you work on, you may find that new CSS becomes usable far faster than you might expect.

It's all too easy to make assumptions about browser support based on something we knew to be true ten years ago. If you're starting a new project now, test those assumptions. If this is a redesign, look at the analytics for the site. Which browser versions are people using? Crucially, which features do those browsers support? You may be surprised, and that data can help you plan your implementation.

You can import Google Analytics data into caniuse.com (http://bkaprt.com/ncl/07-01/) to see how your data weighs up against global or local data (**FIG 7.1**).

If you don't have an existing site to mine data from, look at the global or local statistics and then combine that with your knowledge of the audience for the website. There are certain markets where you find higher usage of older browsers, just as there are places where you will find your audience skewed in terms of newer browsers. Do your research and find out where your project fits.

Check mobile support separately

It's a good idea to separate out the statistics for mobile devices and desktops. You may find that the mobile devices typically accessing the site have far better support for new features than desktop computers. This may mean you can use newer features to assist in creating a better and more performant site for your mobile visitors, even if you need to use older methods in desktop-focused CSS.

Convincing your client or boss

This is all very well, you may be thinking, *but my client expects the site to look identical in these older browsers*. My suggestion is to move the conversation away from "looks the same" to talk about development more holistically. The way the site "looks" is just one aspect of a site; it just so happens that it's the easiest for the client to understand, so they naturally focus on it. By helping them understand that there are lots of elements at play and several trade-offs to be made, you can help them become more informed about the full picture. It's also worth digging into why they are focused on the site "looking the same." What is their underlying concern?

Perhaps your client is concerned about search engines. Can they access the site? In response, you can talk about how mod-

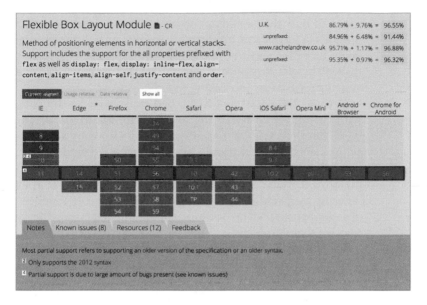

FIG 7.1: caniuse.com shows that visitors to my personal website have better-than-average support for flexbox.

ern search engines care about performance and mobile-friendliness. Newer layout methods can assist in making a search-engine-friendly site.

Or maybe your client worries that their brand identity will get lost in a version of the site tailored to less capable browsers. Some concrete examples may help illustrate how you would make sure users running older browsers will still get a consistent experience of your client's brand and visual style. Here, you can draw parallels with responsive design. A site viewed on a phone differs from the same site viewed on the desktop, yet it still conveys the appropriate identity and visual style—tailored for the way it is being viewed. Older browsers are limited to some extent, but can nevertheless be provided with a good experience that will work well with their constraints.

Your client may also be very budget-conscious. If that's the case, you can talk about how newer methods are faster in development and likely to create a site that is more future-proof; or how they could spend more money to get a site that is identical in IE9 and modern browsers, but that the money might be better spent on advertising or adding some features that will help more visitors convert. Help them see your advice as being focused on protecting their budget.

Perhaps the client has had a bad experience in the past, with customers complaining that the site doesn't work for them. Put their mind at ease by explaining how, by serving a simpler layout to older browsers, they are less likely to run into these issues. Visitors with older browsers will get a fast and performant website, tailored to the device they have. That's a far better proposition than trying to somehow create a modern experience using old technology, something that is more likely to cause them problems.

If you've already done your research, you'll have data to back this up. You can show figures and compare those to other decisions the client makes that also potentially exclude sections of the audience from the "full" experience. The client can then start to understand that the way the site "looks" is not the full story, and you can work together to make sure the site meets the goals of the business.

PROGRESSIVE ENHANCEMENT WITH CSS FEATURE QUERIES

You've looked at the data, you've argued the case for browser support to your client, and you've come to the decision that it makes sense to use features of CSS Grid Layout in your project. How should you go about ensuring that the percentage of users who do not have Grid Layout support can use the site, too?

CSS provides an answer to this question in the shape of *feature queries*. Feature queries are part of the CSS Conditional Rules Module (http://bkaprt.com/ncl/07-02/), the module that also includes media queries. If you've ever used a media query, feature queries will seem very familiar.

Feature queries are created by using the `@supports` rule, just as media queries use `@media`. When we use a feature query, rather than testing for support of a screen size or type of media, we test for support of a CSS feature. The basic syntax is as follows:

```
@supports (display: grid) {
  // code only for browsers that support CSS Grid
  layout
  .container {
  display: grid;
  }
}
```

We start with @supports; then, inside the brackets, we add the property and value we want to test for. Note that this works for prefixed properties, too. To check to see if the browser supports the legacy Internet Explorer implementation (which would give you current Edge browsers), you could use this:

```
@supports (display: -ms-grid) { }
```

You can test for multiple properties and values. For example, to test for support for either the modern CSS Grid specification *or* the earlier one in Edge, use the following:

```
@supports (display: grid) or (display: -ms-grid) { }
```

You could look for a browser that supports more than one feature:

```
@supports (display: grid) and (shape-outside:
  circle(50%)) { }
```

All of our modern browsers support feature queries, which means you can use them to detect and then write code for any new feature that lands in CSS from this point on. That code will be safely tucked away inside your @supports rule, so it won't be executed by browsers that don't have support—they won't understand the rule and therefore will throw the CSS away.

The approach to take with feature queries is to layer on support in a progressively enhanced way. Write CSS for the simplest case, for the browsers with no support. Then layer on features, wrapping that code in a feature query. You'll need to do some overwriting of earlier code inside those feature queries; because of the way CSS works, however, overwriting earlier layout methods for Grid and flexbox is easier than you might think.

Do you need to use a feature query at all?

Before using a feature query, check to see whether you *need* to use one. In CSS, if a browser doesn't understand a feature, it simply throws the CSS away. This means that a lot of progressive enhancement involves writing old CSS, then writing the new CSS afterward, exploiting the fact that later CSS will overwrite earlier CSS in your stylesheet.

Feature queries are necessary whenever you want to include CSS to go along with the Grid or flexbox display—for example, decoration that only makes sense when an item is a grid item. In such cases, you'll want to wrap the CSS in a feature query to prevent anything in that block from being executed. You might also use a feature query to overwrite something used as styling for older browsers that is either not necessary or would badly interact with the display when used in conjunction with the new CSS. The next few examples will examine both cases.

Overwriting floats

The specifications detail how flexbox and Grid interact with other layout methods. For both flexbox and Grid, the specification explains that float and clear have no effect on a flex or Grid item. This means that if you float an item, then make it a flex or Grid item, the float will have no effect.

In my next example, I have a set of floated items. The layout they create will work for all browsers, but has the issues that we explored in Chapter 1: uneven amounts of content can break the layout.

In addition to the float CSS, I've added rules that make the ul a flex container and assign the flex properties to the list items:

```
.cards {
  display: flex;
  flex-wrap: wrap;
}
.cards li {
  /* float for older browsers */
  float: left;
  width: calc(33.333333333% - 20px);
  /* flex for newer ones*/
  flex: 1 1 auto;
}
```

Code example: http://bkaprt.com/ncl/07-03/

If I want the flex-basis to use the width set on the item for the floated layout, I can set flex-basis to auto. In the previous example, flex-grow is set to 1, so items can grow and shrink from that flex-basis. If two items are on the last row, they split the space (**FIG 7.2**).

You can make flexbox use the width and not grow from that percentage by setting the flex-grow value to 0 and keeping the flex-basis as auto, in which case the width used on the item will be the value of the width property. Alternatively, you can override the width by setting the flex-basis to something else, such as 0. You don't need to use any feature queries in this scenario, since older browsers ignore the flexbox rules; if a browser does use the flexbox rules, these override the float.

If we do the same thing with Grid Layout, we define our grid on the container element as a flexible grid with a flexible number of column tracks, each set to 1fr. We don't need to define anything on the grid items.

```
.cards {
  display: grid;
  grid-template-columns: repeat(auto-fill,
  minmax(250px, 1fr));
}
```

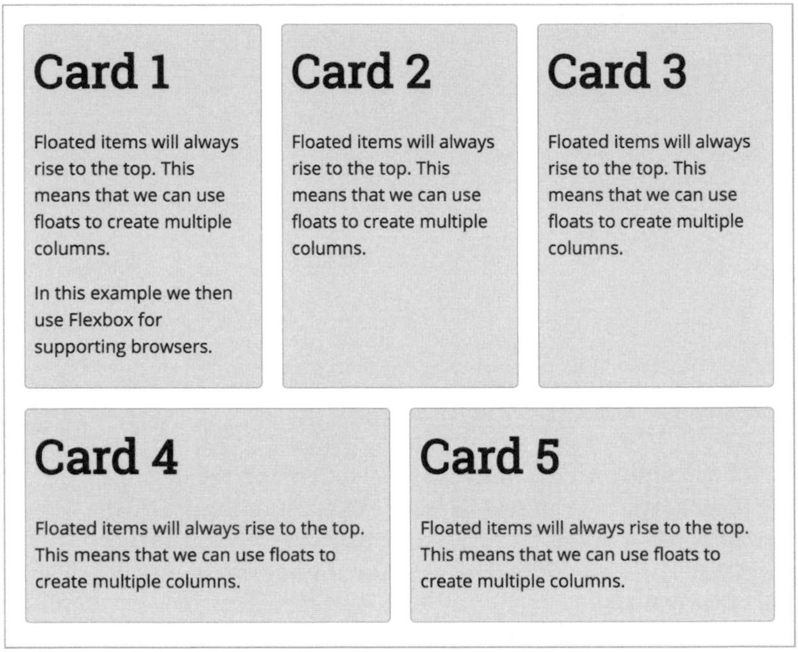

Card 1	**Card 2**	**Card 3**
Floated items will always rise to the top. This means that we can use floats to create multiple columns.

In this example we then use Flexbox for supporting browsers. | Floated items will always rise to the top. This means that we can use floats to create multiple columns. | Floated items will always rise to the top. This means that we can use floats to create multiple columns. |

Card 4	**Card 5**
Floated items will always rise to the top. This means that we can use floats to create multiple columns.	Floated items will always rise to the top. This means that we can use floats to create multiple columns.

FIG 7.2: Items can grow and shrink from a flex-basis of 33.333333333% - 20px.

But there's a problem. While older browsers will ignore the Grid rules, newer browsers that do support Grid will also honor the width we've set on the individual items (**FIG 7.3**).

This is precisely the sort of scenario that might prompt us to reach for a feature query. If we reset the width for our items to auto, the grid layout will work as expected. But we don't want that width to be used for non-supporting browsers. To make sure it won't apply to older browsers, we can wrap that rule in a feature query:

```
@supports (display: grid) {
  .cards li {
    width: auto;
  }
}
```

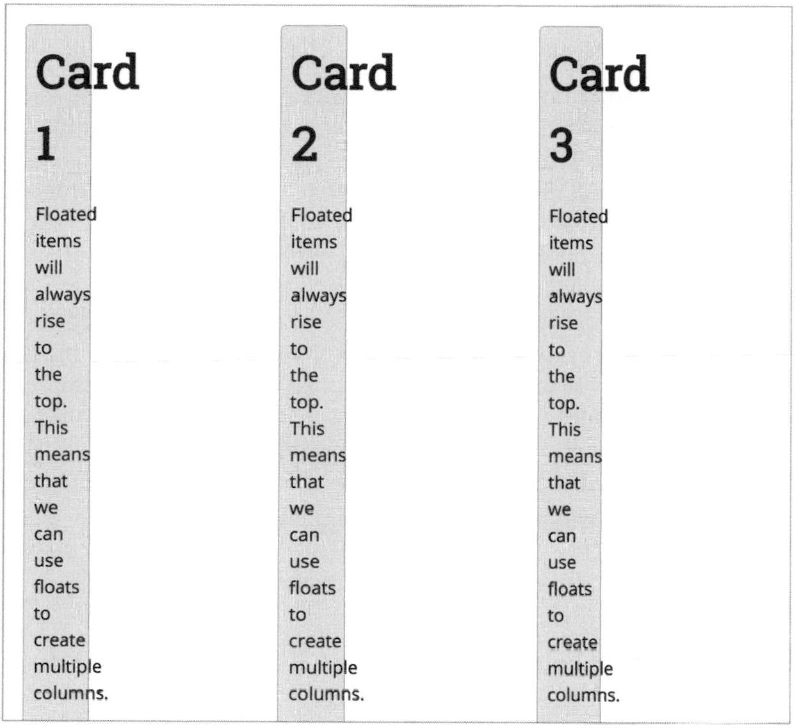

Card 1	Card 2	Card 3
Floated items will always rise to the top. This means that we can use floats to create multiple columns.	Floated items will always rise to the top. This means that we can use floats to create multiple columns.	Floated items will always rise to the top. This means that we can use floats to create multiple columns.

FIG 7.3: The width set on individual items is causing them to become 33.333333333% - 20px of the grid cell.

Code example: http://bkaprt.com/ncl/07-04/

Resetting widths is one of the most common things you will do when creating layouts that work for old and new browsers. Rarely will you need to write two completely different sets of CSS. A lot of the styling of components is the same in both cases; a good amount of the overwriting is done simply by dint of the way CSS works, and the additional rules inside feature queries are there only to adjust small things for the supporting browsers.

Overwriting display: inline-block

In Chapter 1, we looked at some of the other methods we used to create multiple column layouts in browsers prior to flexbox and Grid. We used `display: inline-block` and `display: table`. How do these methods behave if we then override them with flex and Grid?

The good news: they behave in pretty much the same way as our floated example.

Let's revisit the `inline-block` example from Chapter 1 and add flexbox properties to the container and child items. In browsers that support flexbox, the child items become flex items, which negates the `inline-block` behavior—as you can see if you reintroduce white space between the elements. The layout doesn't break, as it did when we tried to use `inline-block` to create a neat grid in Chapter 1.

```
.cards {
  display: flex;
  flex-wrap: wrap;
}
.cards li {
  display: inline-block;
  vertical-align: top;
  width: calc(33.333333333% - 20px);
  flex: 1 1 auto;
}
```

Code example: http://bkaprt.com/ncl/07-05/

Note that the specification explains that `vertical-align` has no effect on flex and Grid items, so this property will not cause a conflict with any alignment properties set to work with flexbox or Grid.

If you perform this override using CSS Grid Layout, it will exhibit the same issue as the floated example above, and you will need to override the width set on the element to prevent issues with your grid.

Overwriting display: table

For `display: table`, how much overwriting we need to do depends on the properties we've used. However, the specification details what happens when an item is set to `display: table-cell` and later the parent is set to `display: grid`.

When we use table properties on things that are not tables, we would quite often use `display: table-cell` on the item itself, without adding any other table properties. As we discovered in Chapter 1, this is one way to create full-height columns, or centering on both axes in browsers, right back to IE8. When doing this, we may not add an element to represent the table row or table itself. A real HTML table does not just contain a `td` in isolation—it requires a `tr` and `table` element to wrap the cells; these elements are necessary for browsers to display a table correctly. For this reason, anonymous elements are created. These fix up the DOM tree, ensuring that our cell has a virtual row and table to display inside. For developers, this behavior is transparent. But what happens if your item set as a table cell becomes a grid item when the parent has `display: grid`?

Thankfully, the specification has you covered. In the next example, I have a three-column layout that uses `display: table-cell` on the individual columns to enable the columns to have equal height visually. I also use the `vertical-align` property to align the table cells, as we can use this alignment method when in a table layout.

```
.cards {
          margin: 0;
          padding: 0;
          list-style: none;
          border-spacing: 20px;

}


    .cards li {
          display: table-cell;
          vertical-align: top;
          padding: 10px;
          border-radius: 5px;
      }
```

Code example: *http://bkaprt.com/ncl/07-06/*

I then add `display: grid` to the parent. In a supporting browser, the grid items are *blockified*, transformed into block elements and not table-cell elements. This transformation happens before the anonymous boxes are created. The items then become grid items. Because the blockification happens before the items become table cells, we get no anonymous boxes created to wrap the items, so our two child elements become two separate grid items. We don't need to worry about isolating the table and grid code from browsers.

```
.cards {
          margin: 0;
          padding: 0;
          list-style: none;
          border-spacing: 20px;
        display: grid;
        grid-template-columns: repeat(3,1fr);
        grid-gap: 20px;
      }
```

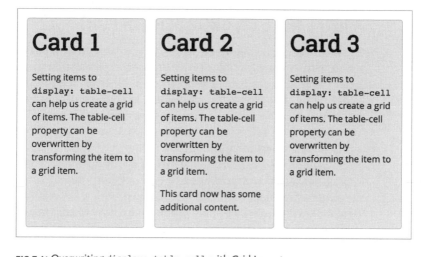

FIG 7.4: Overwriting `display: table-cell` with Grid Layout.

In this scenario, we only need to wrap code in a feature query with @supports if we have something that applies to both grid-supporting and non-grid-supporting browsers. In the table layout, we might use border-spacing to space out the items, which also adds space around the wrapper. For the grid layout, we could replace that by using a margin wrapped in a feature query (**FIG 7.4**).

```
@supports(display: grid) {
  .cards {
  margin: 20px;
  }
}
```

A FINAL NOTE ON BROWSER SUPPORT

Even though you may need to provide a very high level of design consistency for older browsers, don't assume that these newer methods are totally out of reach. Instead of thinking about using them for full-page layout, ask yourself how you might use them to enhance smaller UI elements. Or consider whether your mobile browser profiles enable more use in those small-screen views of your content.

You might also explore using Grid Layout during a prototyping phase. Even if you need to go back and rebuild some elements using older methods once decisions have been made, Grid makes it very easy to play around with how elements will work at various breakpoints. Using it to prototype can help you to really get to grips with the specification, even if business requirements mean it is too early to fully adopt right now.

This book has aimed to explain our newer layout methods, how they fit together, and how you can start using them in your work today. Before I leave you to do that, I'd like to encourage you to participate in the future of CSS. Let's take a look at how to keep up to date with CSS, and how to get involved with pushing it forward.

WHERE ARE WE GOING?

AS WE HAVE SEEN in this book, CSS is changing and developing at a rapid rate. These specifications and features are not developed in a vacuum—while the CSS Working Group discusses and documents how features will work in practice, we can *all* participate in that process. In this chapter, I'll share some exciting developments that I think will become very real possibilities in the not-so-distant future. I'll also explain how you can become involved in the future of the web, and why doing so is important.

UNDERSTANDING CSS VERSIONS

A common misunderstanding about CSS is that the current version of CSS is CSS3, and a future version will be CSS4, and so on. However, if you look at the specifications for flexbox and Grid, you will note that they are both Level 1. What's up with that?

CSS versions 1 and 2 were single monolithic specifications. Each was one massive specification detailing all of CSS. The big change occurred with the version we tend to describe as CSS3: at this point, CSS became modular; the CSS3 modules were essentially all the parts of CSS2.1, split up into separate modules. They could then be worked on individually as version 3 of that part of CSS.

That's why you find Level 3 of the Selectors specification, Level 3 of display, and so forth. These all existed in earlier versions of CSS; the Level 3 version builds on what went before. You will also find some Level 4 specifications, for those mature parts of CSS now moving on past Level 3.

Brand-new CSS, such as Grid and flexbox, starts life at Level 1 because it never existed in the CSS 2 or 2.1 specifications. Since both specifications are now advanced in the process, new features will be proposed for a Level 2, and this is where new work for these specifications will take place.

FOLLOW ALONG WITH THE SPEC

Because CSS is developed in the open, you can track what is going on and make suggestions, too. Since 2016, issues raised against specifications—whether pointing out errors or discussing new features—have happened on GitHub (http://bkaprt. com/ncl/08-01/). You can go to GitHub, read all the issues, and raise your own.

Because discussion around specifications tends to become very technical very quickly, it's unlikely that a suggestion will be immediately dropped into a specification. Fig 8.1, for example, shows how some issues have been marked as `css-grid-2`— meaning that these will be discussed as features in the next level of CSS Grid Layout. Nevertheless, providing a use case for something not currently possible in CSS can spark conversation about a feature for a future version of a specification. It's always worth putting together your thoughts. Don't be discouraged if nothing happens right away—CSS is something of a long game! Remember that the CSS Grid Layout specification was in development as a spec and in browsers for well over five years before it became available in production.

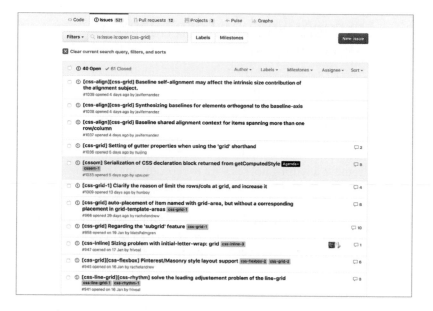

FIG 8.1: The open issues for the CSS Grid Layout specification.

The other place where CSS happens is in the weekly telephone conference of the CSS Working Group and in face-to-face meetings. These meetings are all transcribed and posted into IRC; those notes are then published to the www-style mailing list (http://bkaprt.com/ncl/08-02/). If you want to know what the discussion was around a certain feature—perhaps after seeing the spec issue resolved on GitHub—you can go look in the archives and find the meeting notes.

Following these discussions is an excellent way to learn more about CSS and how features are implemented in browsers. It quickly gives you an appreciation for the work that goes into creating an interoperable web.

ENCOURAGING BROWSER SUPPORT AND LOGGING BUGS

Speaking of interoperability, the other place where everyone can help move the web forward is in reporting browser bugs and pushing browser vendors to implement features. If you think you've found an issue, put together a test case and report it (http://bkaprt.com/ncl/08-03/). When creating your test case, remove anything not relevant to reproducing the issue. This will not only help you determine that the issue really is a browser problem, but will also ensure that the engineer looking at your issue can quickly see the problem. If you're working with a very new specification, it's quite possible that you've encountered a place where that specification interacts with some other part of CSS in a way that no one else has yet spotted—so do log the things you come across. The people who work on browsers are very keen to hear what we, the community building websites for them, find (**FIG 8.2**).

When it comes to browsers implementing new features, encouraging support for features can be as simple as writing about something you would love to see more support for. Developer interest is one of the key forces driving a feature getting implemented in browsers or being worked on by the CSS Working Group. We can gauge developer interest by searching for tweets, blog posts, articles, and slide decks about a specification. If no one seems interested in a particular feature, it won't be prioritized.

NEW FEATURES ON THE HORIZON

On that note, I can think of quite a few features—some specced and with browser implementations, others just ideas—that I would love to be able to use soon. Perhaps you will find something here to inspire you, too.

L. David Baron
@davidbaron

CSS Grid is now in Firefox (52) Beta. For bugs we need to hear about before shipping, tell us in next 2-3 weeks at bugzilla.mozilla.org/enter_bug.cgi?...

3:05 AM - 26 Jan 2017 · Berkeley, CA

↩ ↻ 50 ♥ 37

FIG 8.2: David Baron from Mozilla tweets about logging bugs in CSS Grid Layout prior to the specification shipping in Firefox.

The future of CSS Grid Layout

CSS Grid Layout gives us abilities we have not had before in CSS. As we all get to grips with what is possible, however, some things are not quite possible *yet*. I'm very keen to see subgrid support, as described in Chapter 6, but there are other interesting possibilities up for discussion. Here are some that have already been raised as issues. If you come up with additional use cases, please write them up!

Styling grid areas

In Level 1 of the Grid Layout specification, there is no concept of being able to style grid cells or areas themselves. You can style a grid item placed in the area, but not the actual area. At the time of writing, there is a proposal on GitHub to add a pseudo-element that would enable the adding of backgrounds and borders to the grid, without needing to insert a redundant element just to do so (http://bkaprt.com/ncl/08-04/). Ultimately, this feature may be implemented in a different way, but the idea is something I would love to see happen.

Creating non-rectangular grid elements

In Level 1, grid areas must be rectangular. Perhaps a future level would enable the creation of areas that were L- or T-shaped. A note appears in the Level 1 specification about this (http://bkaprt.com/ncl/08-05/)—more use cases for such a feature would help in promoting it as an idea in Level 2.

More control over auto-placement

One of the most exciting parts of the Grid Layout specification is the ability to auto-place items into a grid. We have some control over the items, as I described in Chapter 6. What we can't do at present is declare rules to place an item into every other cell, or place items against a certain named grid line.

I think that as people start to use Grid Layout in production, many more use cases for auto-placement will start to emerge. If you have one, don't keep it to yourself. Raise an issue on GitHub to see if other people are interested in that idea, too.

Other specifications

Other specifications related to layout could, in combination with Grid, offer some interesting possibilities.

CSS Regions

The CSS Regions specification has a patchy history (http://bkaprt.com/ncl/08-06/). At one point, it looked as though it would be available in Chrome; then, as Blink and WebKit went their separate ways, the specification was removed from Blink. The specification has received little interest since, despite still being implemented with a -webkit prefix in Safari, and in a slightly different form in Internet Explorer and Edge.

Regions takes a chunk of content, passes it to a layout, and then allows that content to flow through the defined areas of that layout. It would give us the nice ability we have in multiple-column layout, where we can take a complete article and split it into columns. With CSS Grid Layout to create the

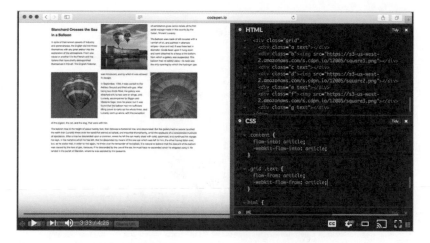

FIG 8.3: A video demonstration of Regions and Grid can be found on my site (http://bkaprt.com/ncl/08-07/).

containers for the content, this could be a powerful way to maintain semantic content while being able to display it creatively (FIG 8.3).

CSS Exclusions

The CSS Shapes specification (which I discussed briefly in Chapter 3) makes it possible to wrap text around non-rectangular shapes. Along with the Regions specification, this specification was originally developed by a team at Adobe. In its original form, it was named Exclusions and Shapes, and contained an interesting idea known as CSS Exclusions (http://bkaprt.com/ncl/08-08/).

The Exclusions part of the specification was removed and placed in a separate specification. There was implementation in IE10 (and this implementation still functions in Edge), but other vendors have shown little interest in implementing this.

Exclusions enables the flowing of text around all sides of an element. An early specification described it as "positioned floats," which is a pretty good description. To create an

CSS Exclusions Example

Lorem ipsum dolor sit amet, consectetur adipiscing elit. Nam posuere quam non enim commodo, ac pellentesque tortor lacinia. Aenean iaculis interdum tempor. Nullam porttitor lectus eget mollis egestas. Cras posuere velit id vehicula tempor. Mauris id ex id nisi sagittis ornare vitae a erat. Aliquam nisi risus, gravida sit amet augue id, feugiat tempor dui. Vestibulum tincidunt iaculis tellus, eget finibus odio.

Quisque ac dapibus massa. Donec sagittis turpis lobortis ac. Praesent velit, id placerat enim imperdiet sit consequat ligula tellus, quis lacinia Praesent sit amet faucibus purus. augue.  placerat nisi velit, quis ornare malesuada amet. Vestibulum mauris porta in. Integer vel sagittis

Aliquam tempor interdum volutpat. Nunc nibh elit, sagittis nec libero a, sapien. Aliquam eu risus eu dui Suspendisse potenti. pretium fermentum varius elementum. Curabitur ut ex luctus, egestas dui sit amet, malesuada lectus. Cras a nibh in velit mattis feugiat at at eros. Etiam et leo arcu. Maecenas egestas enim purus, at ornare velit laoreet a. Etiam egestas pharetra diam, non accumsan sapien posuere ornare. Ut sed velit porttitor dolor tincidunt tincidunt. Pellentesque sit amet pulvinar diam. Cras et purus vulputate, consequat dui vel, cursus risus. Quisque pulvinar convallis tempor. Lorem ipsum dolor sit amet, consectetur adipiscing elit.

Sed mollis fermentum lorem, vel vulputate lectus lacinia sit amet. Praesent pulvinar ante id consequat cursus. Quisque faucibus dui et massa suscipit, nec hendrerit nulla ornare. Donec accumsan eros a dictum tempor. Vestibulum a metus id quam eleifend ornare. Fusce sit amet lacus ut nisi viverra volutpat ultrices a ipsum. Ut lacus leo, dictum sit amet nulla ac, volutpat tempor nunc. Donec ut enim eget massa luctus finibus ac ac lorem. Vestibulum pretium lacus a orci molestie volutpat quis eget mi. Aenean lacus erat, dignissim eget mollis auctor, vehicula a dolor. Curabitur id mollis eros, at auctor ipsum.

FIG 8.4: An "exclusion" with text wrapped around the image.

Exclusion, you position an element using another positioning method—Grid Layout, or even absolute positioning—and then add the property wrap-flow to flow content around all sides you would use:

```
.item {
    wrap-flow: both;
}
```

Fig 8.4 shows the effect that this can create, and I have more details on using Exclusions on my own site (http://bkaprt.com/ncl/08-09/).

These are just a couple of the interesting specifications that are part of the current list of possibilities for CSS. The CSS Working Group Current Work page is a good place to start exploring what else might be upcoming, or at least up for discussion (http://bkaprt.com/ncl/08-10/).

YOU AND THE FUTURE OF THE WEB

As I wrap up this chapter, and this book, I hope that I leave you with a clearer understanding of layout today. I also hope that I inspire you to become involved in creating the open standards that we all use to develop sites and applications.

Much of the understanding I have of CSS, and of the web in general, has come by way of following specification discussions, reading the specs, and then trying to distill what I know into articles and books like this one. I'm not a browser engineer; I'm a web developer with no formal training. But I have an unflagging curiosity that has lasted my twenty years in this business about how these things work, and a passion for making things better. I have learned so much through experimenting with new CSS. I have become a better developer by asking questions, offering my opinion, and sometimes finding out just how hard creating CSS that won't break existing websites really is!

If I can leave you with any advice, it is to make room for time to play with new things. Use your personal projects or just play in an environment like CodePen or JS Bin. Poke at the edges of what is possible. When things don't seem to work the way you think they should, ask questions. Listen to the answers, but don't be afraid to share your ideas and use cases. The people building browsers and editing specifications aren't building production websites in most cases. You are. Your voice is important.

RESOURCES

You will find resources mentioned throughout this book. This list contains material I've created, the references I use in my own work, and resources I would recommend for further exploration of CSS layout.

- **Grid by Example**. I started this site to collect the small examples I was creating as I learned the CSS Grid specification. It is now a resource that includes many examples and patterns, and a video tutorial to help you learn CSS Grid Layout (http://bkaprt.com/ncl/09-01/).
- **CSS Layout News**. My weekly roundup of useful and interesting CSS-layout-related things (http://bkaprt.com/ncl/09-02/).
- **Mozilla Web Docs: Grid Layout**. I wrote the CSS Grid documentation for the Mozilla documentation site. If you enjoy learning by reading and looking at examples, you should find this useful (http://bkaprt.com/ncl/09-03/).
- **Using Feature Queries in CSS**. An article by Jen Simmons explaining how to best use feature queries to provide fallback layouts (http://bkaprt.com/ncl/09-04/).
- **The Experimental Layout Lab of Jen Simmons**. A collection of experiments and examples of web layout (http://bkaprt.com/ncl/09-05/).

- **GridBugs.** I'm curating a list of interoperability issues in Grid Layout. If you think you may be dealing with a browser bug, check the list for help (http://bkaprt.com/ncl/09-06/).
- **Flexbugs.** My GridBugs site was inspired by this repository of flexbox issues and workarounds (http://bkaprt.com/ncl/09-07/).
- **CSS Grid Layout.** A video of my talk at An Event Apart. Although this talk was recorded prior to Grid shipping in browsers, the information about Grid Layout is all still completely valid (http://bkaprt.com/ncl/09-08/).
- **Is It Really Safe to Start Using CSS Grid Layout?** Thoughts on starting to use Grid Layout, and how to do so in a way that doesn't cut off users of older browsers from your site (http://bkaprt.com/ncl/09-09/).
- **Grid Fallbacks and Overrides Cheatsheet.** How to use Grid Layout to overwrite older layout methods (http://bkaprt.com/ncl/09-10/).
- **Box Alignment Cheatsheet.** How to align things in Grid and flexbox (http://bkaprt.com/ncl/09-11/).
- **The Complete Guide to Flexbox.** A flexbox cheat sheet on CSS Tricks (http://bkaprt.com/ncl/09-12/).
- **Flexbox Froggy.** A game to help you learn flexbox (http://bkaprt.com/ncl/09-13/).
- **How to Get Started with CSS Shapes.** A walk-through of CSS Shapes, the different options, and how to use them (http://bkaprt.com/ncl/09-14/).
- **What's the Deal with Collapsible Margins?** This often confuses people; here's an excellent explanation by Ire Aderinokun (http://bkaprt.com/ncl/09-15/).

ACKNOWLEDGEMENTS

Thanks to the team at A Book Apart, especially Katel LeDû, Lisa Maria Martin, and Caren Litherland, for helping shape my stream of thoughts about layout into a book. Thanks, too, to Chen Hui Jing, who, in her capacity as technical editor, ensured that those thoughts were technically correct.

A special thanks to my friend and conference dining companion, Jen Simmons. So many of my thoughts about CSS have been informed by our conversations, as we meet up in cities around the world.

To Jeffrey and Eric, the An Event Apart team, and the travelling collective of speakers: thank you. Thank you for giving me a place to talk about these ideas, and to learn from your wonderful audiences. You have pushed me to be better as a speaker and as a thinker. I will always be grateful for that.

A massive thank you to the CSS Working Group. I'm honored to be a part of this collection of people who are helping to shape what CSS will become. I have learned so much through working with you all, and hope that I can continue to find ways to help shape the future of CSS layout.

While I was writing this book, my daughter graduated from college and started her first professional job. She—like CSS—is twenty years old this year. I am a fortunate person to have her support, along with that of my husband Drew, as I write books, research specs, and vanish down my latest rabbit hole of interest. Thank you; I love you both very much.

REFERENCES

Shortened URLs are numbered sequentially; the related long
URLs are listed below for reference.

Chapter 1

01-01 https://www.thenoodleincident.com/tutorials/box_lesson/boxes.html

01-02 http://alistapart.com/article/fauxcolumns

01-03 http://alistapart.com/article/responsive-web-design

01-04 https://github.com/abookapart/new-css-layout-code/blob/master/chapter1/float.html

01-05 https://github.com/abookapart/new-css-layout-code/blob/master/chapter1/float2.html

01-06 https://github.com/abookapart/new-css-layout-code/blob/master/chapter1/float3.html

01-07 https://github.com/abookapart/new-css-layout-code/blob/master/chapter1/inline-block.html

01-08 https://github.com/abookapart/new-css-layout-code/blob/master/chapter1/display-table.html

Chatper 2

02-01 https://www.smashingmagazine.com/2011/12/an-introduction-to-object-oriented-css-oocss/

02-02 https://smacss.com/

02-03 http://getbem.com/

02-04 http://sass-lang.com

02-05 http://lesscss.org

02-06 https://github.com/postcss/autoprefixer

02-07 http://atomicdesign.bradfrost.com/

02-08 http://patternlab.io/

02-09 http://fractal.build/

02-10 ttp://styleguides.io/

02-11 http://bits.24ways.org

02-12 http://getbootstrap.com/

02-13 http://foundation.zurb.com/

02-14 http://www.httparchive.org/interesting.php?a=All&l=Dec%202%202016

02-15 https://whatdoesmysitecost.com

Chapter 3

03-01 https://drafts.csswg.org/css-display-3/#formatting-context

03-02 https://github.com/abookapart/new-css-layout-code/blob/master/chapter3/bfc.html

03-03 https://github.com/abookapart/new-css-layout-code/blob/master/chapter3/flow-root.html

03-04 https://github.com/abookapart/new-css-layout-code/blob/master/chapter3/flow.html

03-05 https://github.com/abookapart/new-css-layout-code/blob/master/chapter3/float-list.html

03-06 https://github.com/abookapart/new-css-layout-code/blob/master/chapter3/float-shapes.html

03-07 https://github.com/abookapart/new-css-layout-code/blob/master/chapter3/position-absolute.html

03-08 https://github.com/abookapart/new-css-layout-code/blob/master/chapter3/position-fixed.html

03-09 https://github.com/abookapart/new-css-layout-code/blob/master/chapter3/position-sticky.html

03-10 https://github.com/abookapart/new-css-layout-code/blob/master/chapter3/multicolumn-layout.html

03-11 https://github.com/abookapart/new-css-layout-code/blob/master/chapter3/flexbox.html

03-12 https://github.com/abookapart/new-css-layout-code/blob/master/chapter3/flexbox-wrap.html

03-13 https://github.com/abookapart/new-css-layout-code/blob/master/chapter3/flexbox-grid.html

03-14 https://github.com/abookapart/new-css-layout-code/blob/master/chapter3/grid-basics.html

03-15 https://github.com/abookapart/new-css-layout-code/blob/master/chapter3/grid-basics-gaps.html

03-16 https://github.com/abookapart/new-css-layout-code/blob/master/chapter3/grid-basics-lines.html

03-17 https://github.com/abookapart/new-css-layout-code/blob/master/chapter3/grid-basics-areas.html

Chapter 4

04-01   https://drafts.csswg.org/css-align/

04-02   https://github.com/abookapart/new-css-layout-code/blob/master/chapter4/flexbox-align.html

04-03   https://github.com/abookapart/new-css-layout-code/blob/master/chapter4/flexbox-align-self.html

04-04   https://github.com/abookapart/new-css-layout-code/blob/master/chapter4/flexbox-align-columns.html

04-05   https://github.com/abookapart/new-css-layout-code/blob/master/chapter4/grid-align.html

04-06   https://hacks.mozilla.org/2016/12/css-grid-and-grid-highlighter-now-in-firefox-developer-edition/

04-07   https://github.com/abookapart/new-css-layout-code/blob/master/chapter4/grid-align-self.html

04-08   https://github.com/abookapart/new-css-layout-code/blob/master/chapter4/grid-justify.html

04-09   https://github.com/abookapart/new-css-layout-code/blob/master/chapter4/flexbox-justify.html

04-10   https://github.com/abookapart/new-css-layout-code/blob/master/chapter4/center.html

04-11   https://github.com/abookapart/new-css-layout-code/blob/master/chapter4/flexbox-align-content.html

04-12   https://github.com/abookapart/new-css-layout-code/blob/master/chapter4/grid-align-content.html

04-13   https://github.com/abookapart/new-css-layout-code/blob/master/chapter4/auto-margins.html

04-14   https://drafts.csswg.org/css-logical-props/

Chapter 5

05-01   https://github.com/abookapart/new-css-layout-code/blob/master/chapter5/flexbox-equal.html

05-02   https://github.com/abookapart/new-css-layout-code/blob/master/chapter5/grid-auto-fill.html

05-03   https://github.com/abookapart/new-css-layout-code/blob/master/chapter5/grid-auto-fill-minmax.html

05-04   https://github.com/abookapart/new-css-layout-code/blob/master/chapter5/grid-auto-fill-v-auto-fit.html

05-05   https://drafts.csswg.org/css-flexbox/#flex-components

05-06   https://github.com/abookapart/new-css-layout-code/blob/master/chapter5/flexbox-flex-basis.html

05-07   https://github.com/abookapart/new-css-layout-code/blob/master/chapter5/flexbox-auto.html

05-08   https://github.com/abookapart/new-css-layout-code/blob/master/chapter5/grid-fr.html

05-10   https://github.com/abookapart/new-css-layout-code/blob/master/chapter5/grid-auto-tracks.html

05-11   https://github.com/abookapart/new-css-layout-code/blob/master/chapter5/grid-auto-rows-minmax.html

Chapter 6

06-01   https://github.com/abookapart/new-css-layout-code/blob/master/chapter6/flex-direction.html

06-02   https://github.com/abookapart/new-css-layout-code/blob/master/chapter6/grid-auto-flow-column.html

06-03   https://github.com/abookapart/new-css-layout-code/blob/master/chapter6/grid-auto-flow-spans.html

06-04   http://tink.uk/flexbox-the-keyboard-navigation-disconnect/

06-05   https://github.com/abookapart/new-css-layout-code/blob/master/chapter6/flex-order.html

06-06   https://drafts.csswg.org/css-grid/#grid-item-placement-algorithm

06-07   https://drafts.csswg.org/css-display/#box-generation

06-08   https://github.com/abookapart/new-css-layout-code/blob/master/chapter6/grid-display-contents.html

Chapter 7

07-01   http://caniuse.com/#stats_import

07-02   https://www.w3.org/TR/css3-conditional

07-03   https://github.com/abookapart/new-css-layout-code/blob/master/chapter7/flex-overrides.html

07-04   ttps://github.com/abookapart/new-css-layout-code/blob/master/chapter7/grid-overrides-float.html

07-05   ttps://github.com/abookapart/new-css-layout-code/blob/master/chapter7/grid-inline-block.html

07-06   https://github.com/abookapart/new-css-layout-code/blob/master/chapter7/display-table.html

Chapter 8

08-01 https://github.com/w3c/csswg-drafts/issues

08-02 https://lists.w3.org/Archives/Public/www-style/

08-03 https://rachelandrew.co.uk/archives/2017/01/30/reporting-browser-bugs/

08-04 https://github.com/w3c/csswg-drafts/issues/499

08-05 https://www.w3.org/TR/css-grid-1/#grid-template-areas-property

08-06 https://drafts.csswg.org/css-regions/

08-07 https://rachelandrew.co.uk/archives/2016/03/25/css-grid-and-css-regions

08-08 https://drafts.csswg.org/css-exclusions/

08-09 https://rachelandrew.co.uk/archives/2016/03/16/css-exclusions-and-grid-layout/

08-10 https://www.w3.org/Style/CSS/current-work

Resources

09-01 https://gridbyexample.com

09-02 http://csslayout.news

09-03 https://developer.mozilla.org/en-US/docs/Web/CSS/CSS_Grid_Layout

09-04 https://hacks.mozilla.org/2016/08/using-feature-queries-in-css/

09-05 http://labs.jensimmons.com/

09-06 https://github.com/rachelandrew/gridbugs

09-07 https://github.com/philipwalton/flexbugs

09-08 https://vimeo.com/212961112

09-09 https://rachelandrew.co.uk/archives/2017/07/04/is-it-really-safe-to-start-using-css-grid-layout/

09-10 https://rachelandrew.co.uk/css/cheatsheets/grid-fallbacks

09-11 https://rachelandrew.co.uk/css/cheatsheets/box-alignment

09-12 https://css-tricks.com/snippets/css/a-guide-to-flexbox/

09-13 http://flexboxfroggy.com/

09-14 https://www.webdesignerdepot.com/2015/03/how-to-get-started-with-css-shapes/

09-15 https://bitsofco.de/collapsible-margins/

INDEX

ABOUT A BOOK APART

We cover the emerging and essential topics in web design and development with style, clarity, and above all, brevity—because working designer-developers can't afford to waste time.

COLOPHON

The text is set in FF Yoga and its companion, FF Yoga Sans, both by Xavier Dupré. Headlines and cover are set in Titling Gothic by David Berlow.

 This book was printed in the United States using FSC certified Finch papers.